"Get ready to travel down a moving journey of faith. Through deeply honest and transparent stories, David Sanford takes the reader down life's roads of spiritual and personal crisis filled with potholes, detours, and winding paths. The destination left me challenged, yet wholly encouraged and filled with hope."

MARK MILLER, author of *Experiential Storytelling*

. . . .

"Anyone who writes knows that an author's omnipresence is an illusion. But I'm convinced that David Sanford gets around more than the rest of us. I think God's given him more experiences, more acquaintances, more conversations, and more serendipitous circumstances than most of us mortals. David is on good speaking terms with just about everyone and everything and that list includes suffering, doubt, trials, anxiety, and grief, making him a trusted and wise companion to walk through faith's disillusionments."

RICK JAMES, author of *Jesus Without Religion*

. . . .

"When I'm in the midst of the unwieldy circumstances of life, and then God disappears, I find myself stumbling around with one question on my lips: Am I all alone? David Sanford doesn't simply answer my question; he engages me like a sage friend and mentor. By the end of the book I sense that God's love for me is more generous and more sturdy than I suspected. Ultimately, *If God Disappears* is a meaningful conversation about hope."

TAMARA PARK, pastor of community, Warehouse 242

. . . .

"If you're more human than religious, this book is for you. If you've ever been hit in the face with life, this book is for you. And if you think God can't take your anger, this book is definitely for you. Real people, real problems, real God. Great book."

SALLY MORGENTHALER, author of *Emergent Manifesto of Hope*, www.shapevine.com

. . . .

"*If God Disappears* shows us how God is always present in love and grace, even when heartache and suffering veils God from our awareness. From the pages of Scripture to the everyday lives of ordinary people, David Sanford uncovers a real faith, capable of sustaining and transforming us through hardship, even in times when we can't see or feel God in our lives."

JIM PALMER, author of *Divine Nobodies* and *Wide Open Spaces*

. . . .

"Most of us have wrestled with the difficult questions this book addresses. The author's honest approach features engaging stories and thoughtful discussion that ultimately lead to hope. A tough topic that is handled with intellect and grace."

DAVE BURCHETT, Emmy Award-winning director for FOX Sports Net and author of *When Bad Christians Happen to Good People*

. . . .

"For anyone who has ever felt abandoned, lonely, deserted . . . those times when it feels even your prayers go unheard . . . this book is for you. All of us need to be reminded that even in the darkest corners of life, God is there. In his book, *If God Disappears*, David Sanford rekindles our hope and strengthens our courage to hang on to what we know in our hearts is absolute and true about the mysterious ways of our loving heavenly Father, even when life goes terribly wrong."

WILLIAM CARMICHAEL, best-selling author and speaker

. . . .

"Doubts about God and ourselves sidetrack so many of us on our faith journey. *If God Disappears* raises honest questions, involves heartfelt stories, and offers practical, biblical wisdom to help us move from denial and despair to devotion to Jesus Christ. David Sanford rightly encourages us not to lose hope but to keep pressing on, remembering that God has a way of showing up—even when we think he's disappeared."

PAUL LOUIS METZGER, PhD, professor of Christian theology and theology of culture, Multnomah Biblical Seminary

. . . .

"Jesus said, 'In this world you will have trouble.' We discover what we really believe by how we respond to an unexpected crisis. Many, like David Sanford, 'lose their faith' in times of testing, only to find an unshakeable foundation in a deeper awareness of God's character, sufficiency, and strength. Take the journey to a deeper faith through reading this book."

MOIRA BROWN, cohost of *100 Huntley Street*

. . . .

"*If God Disappears* is one of the most important books of the year. We all have gone through our own crises of faith and the resulting guilt that goes with it. After reading about the nine 'faith wreckers' and the nine 'faith builders,' your life will never be the same."

PAT WILLIAMS, senior vice president, Orlando Magic, and author of *The Pursuit*

. . . .

"I am so glad I read *If God Disappears*. This is a book about stories—powerful and personal and challenging. These honest stories face head-on the hard and hurting things in life. David Sanford touches your heart and brings you closer to God, no matter what your journey has been."

DR. STEVE STEPHENS, psychologist and best-selling author of *Risking Faith*

. . . .

IF GOD DISAPPEARS

FAITH

AND WHAT
TO DO

ECKERS

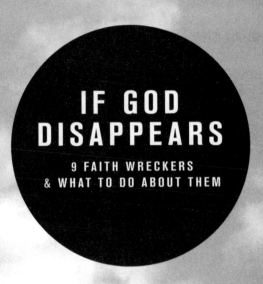

IF GOD DISAPPEARS

9 FAITH WRECKERS
& WHAT TO DO ABOUT THEM

DAVID SANFORD

ABOUT THEM

SALTRIVER®

An Imprint of Tyndale House Publishers, Inc., Carol Stream, Illinois

Visit Tyndale's exciting Web site at www.tyndale.com

TYNDALE is a registered trademark of Tyndale House Publishers, Inc.

SaltRiver and the SaltRiver logo are registered trademarks of Tyndale House Publishers, Inc.

If God Disappears: Nine Faith Wreckers and What to Do about Them

Copyright © 2008 by Sanford Communications, Inc. All rights reserved.

Cover photo copyright © by Veer. All rights reserved.

Author photo copyright © 2008 by Damon Evans. All rights reserved.

Designed by Beth Sparkman

Published in association with the literary agency of Credo Communications LLC, Grand Rapids, MI 49525; www.credocommunications.net.

Unless otherwise indicated, all Scripture quotations are taken from the *Holy Bible*, New Living Translation, copyright © 1996, 2004, 2007 by Tyndale House Foundation. Used by permission of Tyndale House Publishers, Inc., Carol Stream, Illinois 60188. All rights reserved. References for Scripture quotations appear in the Scripture Index on pages 159 and 160.

Scripture quotations marked NIV are taken from the HOLY BIBLE, NEW INTERNATIONAL VERSION®. NIV®. Copyright © 1973, 1978, 1984 by International Bible Society. Used by permission of Zondervan. All rights reserved.

To protect the privacy of those who have shared their stories with the author, some details and names have been changed. Still, every story in this book is true. At the request of several individuals who have told me about their experiences of abuse, one story is a composite.

Library of Congress Cataloging-in-Publication Data

Sanford, David (David R.)
    If God disappears : nine faith wreckers and what to do about them / David Sanford.
        p. cm.
    Includes bibliographical references and index.
    ISBN-13: 978-1-4143-1617-8 (hc : alk. paper)
    ISBN-10: 1-4143-1617-8 (hc : alk. paper)
    1. Faith.   2. Spiritual life—Christianity.   I. Title.
BV4637.S323 2008
234'.23—dc22   2008017285

Printed in the United States of America

14   13   12   11   10   09   08

7   6   5   4   3   2   1

To those who have walked away from faith,
to those who know the day God left them . . .
to those who allowed me to tell their stories,
to those who still welcome me as a friend.

"Most of faith is patience."
John Van Diest

"We read to know we are not alone."
C. S. Lewis

*"It is what we know already that often
prevents us from learning."*
Claude Bernard

*"The heart that breaks open can
contain the whole universe."*
Joanna Macy

*"The human spirit is stronger than
anything that can happen to it."*
George C. Scott

*"Character cannot be developed in ease
and quiet. Only through experience of trial
and suffering can the soul be strengthened,
ambition inspired, and success achieved."*
Helen Keller

*"At every crisis in one's life, it is absolute salvation
to have some sympathetic friend to whom you can
think aloud without restraint or misgiving."*
Woodrow Wilson

*"One who faces his own failures is steadily
advancing on the pilgrim's way."*
William Temple

"Deepest communion with God is beyond words, on the other side of silence."
MADELEINE L'ENGLE

"Prayer and love are learned in the hour when prayer becomes impossible and your heart has turned to stone."
THOMAS MERTON

"Faith is hanging on very stubbornly to the belief that things are not really as they seem."
OSWALD CHAMBERS

"God is not a deceiver, that he should offer to support us, and then, when we lean upon him, should slip away from us."
AUGUSTINE

"To our questions God has provided answers; not all the answers, certainly, but enough to satisfy our intellects and ravish our hearts."
A. W. TOZER

"I am still amazed at how big, how enormous a love and mystery God is . . ."
BONO, U2 SUPERSTAR

CONTENTS

INTRODUCTION

Sometimes it takes the experience of losing someone to shake us out of complacency.

I lost someone when I was eleven. My dad and mom and brother and two sisters and I were near Snoqualmie Pass, about fifty miles east of Seattle.

Waiting in line near the top of the mountain slope was a girl about my age with a new, red snow saucer. Compared to my black, smelly inner tube, it was high tech.

I'd never seen anyone fly so fast down the mountain before. I continued to watch the girl as I made my own way down at less than breakneck speed. Most kids stopped shortly after the slope flattened out. But this girl just kept going and going. And then she disappeared.

I swung around quickly to my left, to my right. Everyone around me was getting up and trudging back up the hill. But I didn't see the girl. She had been right in front of me. And then she was gone.

No one believed me.

I insisted I had seen her disappear. "We can't just walk away. Come back. Help me look for her."

Still no one believed. Except me.

The snow was wet and heavy that day. Off the beaten track, I soon found my boots sinking deeper and deeper into the snowpack. It took a full minute to cover ten yards. But I would not stop. Looking carefully, I could see the slight depression where the girl's red saucer had flown across the surface of the snow.

Scattered alpine trees stuck out of the snow just ahead of me. I looked back and realized I was well off the beaten track. But I knew I had seen the girl go this far.

My heart stopped when I found the dark hole. There, in front of me, the saucer's track stopped.

I lay on the snow with my head sticking out over the hole. The second I heard her crying, I started yelling. "Are you all right? Don't worry. I'll get help. I promise—I'll be back right away."

I didn't have time to go all the way back up the slope to my parents, so I accosted the first adult I found and breathlessly told him my story. He started yelling, and other adults came running. Someone called up the slope, and within minutes someone else was running toward us with a rope.

I led everyone along the path I had taken earlier. It took a while, but eventually a very wet and cold girl was fished out of the creek fourteen feet below the snowpack. She was reunited with her father, and all was well again.

For a long time afterward I pondered what would have happened if I had been the one riding the red saucer.

I also wondered why it was so hard to get anyone to believe me.

The fact is, sometimes the bottom does fall out from under us, God seems to disappear, and it's almost impossible to get anyone to believe us.

I believe you.

EVERYONE HAS A STORY.

What's yours? Have you ever reached a point in your life where God seemed to disappear? Have you ever felt as if things couldn't get any worse? As if someone has turned out the lights and God just slipped away?

Martin Luther called this *Anfechtung*. Saint John of the Cross called it the "dark night of the soul." Only it doesn't usually last a night. It can last for days. Weeks. Months. Even longer.

And when God steps back into the picture, it often feels too late.

Throughout literature, music, and movies, we see the themes of God's (or gods') abandonment, the hero(ine)'s resultant agnosticism, and the immense struggles that ensue. In real life, there's not always a happy ending.

LONG GONE

Remember *Superman Returns*? By the time our messiah-like superhero shows up, five years after disappearing unexpectedly, Lois Lane has won a Pulitzer for her op-ed piece, "Why the World Doesn't Need Superman."

Just when Lois thinks she's completely processed her pain and suffering, she faces a second crisis: Can she make room in her life for Superman again?

Like the shaken believer who feels that God walked away without even waving good-bye, Lois has to decide: Does she even want him back?

We all need to answer that question at some point. Do I want God back?

This is the central question to those who feel God has walked out on them. Everyone has faced—or will face—such crises of faith. For some reason beyond our human understanding, such crises are part of everyone's spiritual journey.

Of course, Superman did return to Lois. But for Christians, sometimes it seems impossible to wait when we have no idea whether or not God is ever coming back. In the darkest times—the death of a close friend or loved one, a horrible accident, acts of terrorism and war, natural disasters, and other tragedies—he seems infinitely far away.

When I was nineteen, a close family friend, Darrell, fell victim to intense headaches. A CAT scan technician first spotted the problem: a massive tumor. Brain surgery followed. Darrell was practically my adopted brother, so I visited him every day. The first day he looked pretty roughed up, but the nurses said he was doing fine. As is customary after such surgeries, they were checking on him every thirty minutes, which was reassuring.

The second day Darrell looked about the same.

The third day his bed was empty. His mother stood in the corner of the room, weeping. Two hours earlier, the nurse on duty had been in to check on Darrell, only to discover he had stopped breathing. The hospital staff rushed to revive him, and now was desperately fighting for his life.

Darrell's mother looked up as I entered the room. Seven years earlier, her first husband and oldest son had died in a tragic boating accident. She then married Darrell's stepfather, but two years later, he had a fatal heart attack. Now this.

She looked down to her right. I'm not even sure she was talking to me. If she was, she certainly wasn't expecting me to say anything in reply.

In her anger she demanded, "Doesn't God know I've suffered enough?"

She was absolutely exhausted. The attending physician came into the room and said there was nothing more they could do. Still in shock, Darrell's mother left.

"Darrell's situation is serious," the doctor told me. "It appears he stopped breathing for fifteen, maybe twenty, minutes. We can't pick up any brain waves. But I don't want to unplug him until we've tried everything we can. Would you sit with Darrell and talk with him? If you get him to respond in any way—a word, a motion, a blink—we'll keep him alive."

The doctor took me to Darrell's room in ICU. For three days, I stayed with Darrell. I talked with him. I stroked his hand. I pleaded with him to let me know he was still there. I desperately looked for any sign of life.

Nothing.

After three days, they turned off life support.

I never realized how powerless I was until that experience. Not only was I unable to save my friend, but I also had nothing to say to his mother in her moment of deepest grief.

Where was God?

Where was *anyone* when Darrell's mom and I felt overwhelmed with such intense feelings of loss and grief?

Who could blame her or me for feeling abandoned?

In the face of unspeakable suffering and pain, why would *anyone* still believe in God? When asked what they would like to ask God if given the opportunity, 44 percent of Americans said they want to know why there is evil or suffering in this world.[1]

FAITH WRECKER · **Experiencing evil and suffering**

GIVING UP

Sarah's hard-driving husband, Rob, wasn't a kind man. Twenty-six long years had proved that beyond a doubt. Day after day, night after night, Sarah prayed for Rob to find God and turn his life around.

But the years had taken their toll, and most of the time Sarah found it to be almost a relief when Rob left the house to go to work. She couldn't remember the last time he had told her good-bye, let alone offered a kiss. That morning was no different, it seemed. Until a knock at the door shortly before lunch. Rob had been headed north on I-5 just outside Sacramento when a semi jackknifed in front of him. A second semi and Rob's hotel shuttle van hit simultaneously, rocketing him out of the vehicle. Seventy-five yards away, he writhed in unimaginable pain. By the time the paramedics arrived, he was almost dead. He officially expired at 10:33, less than two miles from a local hospital.

That day, Sarah experientially lost her faith. She had prayed and prayed for her husband's salvation. Where was God when her husband needed him most? And where was God in the midst of her piercing sorrow?

A year later, Sarah answered the phone and a woman asked if her husband had been in a terrible accident. Sarah demanded to know who was calling.

The woman said her name was Tammy. She had been driving

south when she witnessed the accident. Instinctively, she pulled off the freeway as quickly as she could. In the median someone was dying. She couldn't bear to look. Gripping her steering wheel, she argued with God.

Go to him, God told her.

I can't, Tammy argued. *My two children are in the backseat, bundled in their car seats.*

Go.

No! Please, God, no.

Weeping, Tammy pulled the key out of the ignition, looked back at her sleeping children, stepped out of the car, made sure all the doors were locked, saw that traffic was at a complete stop, and started running between cars toward the median. She knelt in the grass amid the broken glass, took the man's bloody hand, and started talking to him. Immediately, he stopped writhing.

"Look at me," Tammy pleaded. "You're hurt very badly. Do you know God?"

He couldn't speak aloud, but he slowly shook his head no.

"Do you want to know God as your Savior right now?"

He nodded.

"Pray with me," Tammy told him.

When she finished the prayer, Rob squeezed Tammy's hand. "Did you pray with me?" He squeezed again.

Only at that point did Tammy realize a group of people were standing in a circle around her and Rob. Tammy stood up and an off-duty paramedic immediately went to work. The next day Tammy learned that Rob had died before reaching the hospital. After Tammy finished her story, Sarah scoffed. "Why didn't you call me before now? No matter. I don't even believe in God anymore."

Tammy protested, but Sarah rebuffed her. "Don't go quoting Scripture at me. It's not true. God doesn't work all things together for good. My life's ruined."

Sarah told me the same thing. After all the depression and anxiety and stress she'd experienced, her life felt shattered. To this day, she believes God might as well stay put in heaven. She's not looking for him anymore. At least not yet. But God hasn't given up on her. Neither have I.

It's startling to realize the implications of God's unconditional love, grace, and mercy. Like the Prodigal Son's father, God isn't disillusioned with us. He never had any illusions to begin with.

Of course, even if someone knew God wasn't angry at her, if she knew beyond a doubt that God had no intention of heaping guilt or shame on her, there's no guarantee she would turn back to God.

I walked away, didn't I? I made my choice. My fate is sealed, isn't it?

TOO LATE?

The course of your life could change today based on a single decision you'll make—either to open the door of your heart and invite God to come back in or to consciously lock him out of your life forever.

Maybe you have been taught that it's impossible to come back to God. You may have felt God wouldn't take you back anyway. But it's not too late.

Right before the start of World War I, a young French boy named Jean-Paul Sartre and his widowed mother were living with her parents. The grandfather was a Protestant, the grandmother a lifelong French Catholic. At the dinner table, the family patriarch and matriarch often poked fun at the other's religious beliefs.

"I concluded from these exchanges that the two faiths were equally valueless," Jean-Paul later said. "Even though my family saw it as their duty to bring me up as a Catholic, religion never had any weight with me."

By the time the war ended, Jean-Paul had grown completely disenchanted with the church. By the time he turned twelve, he thoroughly hated to attend Mass and resolved that he would go no more.

To seal his decision, Jean-Paul stood before a mirror, stared at his reflection, and then cursed God. He felt a sense of relief. He was through with God and the church. He decided to become an atheist so he could live the rest of his days as he pleased.

Over the years, Sartre looked back at that event as a defining moment in his life. In *Being and Nothingness*, writing against certain Christian beliefs, he commented almost as an aside: "We should know for always whether a particular youthful experience had been fruitful or ill-starred, whether a particular crisis of puberty was a caprice or a real pre-formation of my later engagements; the curve of our life would be fixed forever."

In other words: If I really meant it when I cursed God, I thereby set the course of my entire life and have sealed my fate.

Sartre went on to make a name for himself, of course. His political exploits are legendary, his writings definitive of mid-twentieth-century atheistic existentialism. Yet, reviewing his life, Sartre seemed to swing between the extremes of heady pride and sexual liberation on the one hand, and philosophical anguish and personal despair on the other.

On numerous occasions, Sartre stated that there is "no exit" from the human dilemma of trying to live as if God did not exist. "Man is alone," Sartre claimed, abandoned to his own destiny. "Hell is other people." Life is hard, and then you die. Period. My friend Tim Barnhart says, "He was trying to experience life on his own terms. His 'truth,' though depressing and controversial, was nonetheless an exercise in believing." I agree.

Shortly before his death, Sartre relented. The *Nouvel Observateur* records these words: "I do not feel that I am the product of chance, a speck of dust in the universe, but someone who was expected, prepared, prefigured. In short, a being whom only a Creator could put here; and this idea of a creating hand refers to God."[2]

How tragic that Sartre allowed a decision in his youth to overshadow any consideration of God's relevance for nearly six decades.

Although he's considered one of the greatest twentieth-century philosophers, I believe Sartre committed two of this past century's most prevalent errors of thinking.

First, Sartre confused his *feelings* with *reality*. You see this all the time. A man wakes up one morning, rolls over, sees his wife, and realizes he doesn't have any loving feelings for her. This lack of feelings of love shocks him so much he decides it must be the truth. So he acts accordingly, forgetting that love is more than a momentary feeling. In reality, to love is a decision we make over and over again.

Second, Sartre confused an *event* with *fate*. When he cursed God, he felt he had sealed his destiny. There was no looking back, no recognition that he could choose otherwise.[3]

I don't know your particular life story. Yet after talking individually with hundreds of people over the past decade, I find that many people wish, in their heart of hearts, that they could believe God hasn't abandoned them after all.

Maybe you've consciously cursed God. Maybe you've rejected only the church. Maybe you've simply lacked the confidence to say, "God, if you're real, please make yourself real *to me*."

NIGHTMARE

God wants us to know that even when it's humanly impossible to see or feel him, he is always there with us. Sometimes that's hard to believe. But no matter how deeply we bury grief in our souls, it doesn't go away.

Four years ago, Lisa and her family took a brief but much-needed vacation at a beautiful resort outside Phoenix.

During their fifth night there, Lisa was awakened by a horrific nightmare. She dreamed she was a little girl again, just four years old. Her father was tying a gag in her mouth and then binding her hands. While her mother watched, he carried her through the apartment and down the stairway to a waiting car. He put her in the trunk of the car and slammed the lid shut.

Lying in the dark in her hotel room, Lisa trembled in her bed, perspiring all over. Never had she felt such an overwhelming sense of shock, fear, and abandonment. She couldn't stop the unfolding nightmare. She turned on the light. She wept. She cried out to God for deliverance. Finally, in desperation, she woke her husband, Mark, beating his chest as the nightmare continued to play out in her mind: The four-year-old Lisa was drenched with sweat by the time the trunk lid opened again. She was slapped, then carried into what appeared to be a warehouse. Except for the light from a small wood fire, it was dark inside. Lisa's captors laid her next to the fire, only inches away. She tried to roll away, but they kept kicking her back. Finally, when her clothes were almost dry, they forced her to stand up and then stripped her. Then they started filming the unspeakable atrocities that happened next.

What Mark didn't realize that night was that his own nightmare had just begun. It would be months before Lisa was finally diagnosed with dissociative identity disorder, and by that time, her four-year-old self was often Lisa's dominant personality. She no longer knew anything about God, her Christian faith, or even her husband, often emphatically declaring that she wasn't married to him.

Months later, having no idea what had happened, I sat in Lisa and Mark's living room, expressing my genuine concern for their welfare. Thirty-year-old Lisa looked at Mark, nodded her head, and then looked down for a minute. I sat quietly. Finally, her story—their story—started coming out. I immediately quit asking questions. When someone tells their story, I've learned to listen—just listen. I'm convinced that intertwined within every story you'll find God's redemptive presence where you least expect it.

As Lisa told her story that night, she began to see God again for the first time in a long time. She wept tears of joy as she felt his presence. She realized he was in the midst of her story, after all.

The next morning Lisa called to tell me she had slept through the night for the first time in sixteen months. By week's end, four-year-old Lisa had begun reintegrating with thirty-year-old Lisa. She still had a long road of healing ahead of her, but the process of recovery had begun. Today, her marriage and faith have been fully restored. I say that almost matter-of-factly, but for a long time that was anything but a sure thing.

Lisa said it best: "I discovered there's always hope."[4]

Like Lisa, we all have a story. But unless we're broken enough to take the terrible risk of telling someone our story, no matter how dark it is, we may never reconnect with God again this side of eternity.

Remarkably, as Lisa learned, if we do tell our stories to someone who knows God—without demanding answers to that blackest of all questions ("Why?")—guess who shows up, unannounced?

FAITH BUILDER   **Telling my story to a friend who knows God**

REAL LIFE

As a teenager, I must have read through the Psalms a dozen times each year after my father's health fled and poverty pounced upon our once-proud family. I learned firsthand that God indeed cares deeply about the helpless and oppressed, the wounded and despairing.

Perhaps more than any other portion of Scripture, the Psalms tell us about real life.

Over and over again throughout the Psalms we find the psalmist crying out to God in various dire circumstances.

I have so many enemies!
Take away my distress.
Listen to my cry for help.
Go away, all you who do evil.
Save me from my persecutors—rescue me!

In seven out of every ten psalms, the writer is crying out to God for physical salvation, thanking the Lord for sparing his life, reminding himself of the differing fates of the righteous and evil-doers, or renewing his allegiance to God and his Word in the face of rampant wickedness.

During my teens, as my dad lost his eyesight and the financial pressures on our family became increasingly severe, I was driven again and again to the Psalms. Over time, I memorized nearly fifty of them. They renewed my faith in the God of the afflicted and suffering.

Maybe you haven't thought much about the Scriptures for a long time. Yet if the middle of the Bible teaches us anything, it's how to turn to God in times of trouble and pain. I invite you to consider this brief synopsis with specific examples from various psalms.

■ **Call out to the Lord . . .**
O God, listen to my cry!
Hear my prayer! *Psalm 61:1*

. . . and ask for help!
Please, God, rescue me!
Come quickly, LORD, and help me.   *Psalm 70:1*

■ **Tell God about your troubles . . .**
O God, pagan nations have conquered your land,
    your special possession.
They have defiled your holy Temple
and made Jerusalem a heap of ruins. . . .
We are mocked by our neighbors,
an object of scorn and derision to those
    around us.   *Psalm 79:1, 4*

. . . and admit if you feel abandoned or forsaken.
O LORD, how long will this go on?
Will you hide yourself forever?
How long will your anger burn like fire?   *Psalm 89:46*

■ **Describe what you want God to do . . .**
Give us gladness in proportion to our former misery!
Replace the evil years with good.
Let us, your servants, see you work again;
let our children see your glory.
And may the Lord our God show us his approval
and make our efforts successful.
Yes, make our efforts successful!   *Psalm 90:15-17*

. . . and explain why God should act on your behalf.
Let this be recorded for future generations,
so that a people not yet born will praise the
    LORD. . . .
And so the LORD's fame will be celebrated in Zion,
his praises in Jerusalem,

when multitudes gather together
and kingdoms come to worship the LORD.

Psalm 102:18, 21-22

■ **Give a candid appraisal of your enemy . . .**
They surround me with hateful words
and fight against me for no reason.
I love them, but they try to destroy me with accusations
even as I am praying for them!
They repay evil for good,
and hatred for my love. *Psalm 109:3-5*

. . . and ask God to put that foe in his place.
Arise, O LORD, in anger!
Stand up against the fury of my enemies!
Wake up, my God, and bring justice! *Psalm 7:6*

■ **Honestly evaluate your guilt or innocence . . .**
I have chosen to be faithful;
I have determined to live by your regulations.
I cling to your laws.
LORD, don't let me be put to shame! *Psalm 119:30-31*

. . . and confess any known sins.
I have wandered away like a lost sheep;
come and find me,
for I have not forgotten your commands. *Psalm 119:176*

■ **Affirm your implicit trust in God . . .**
I look up to the mountains—
does my help come from there?
My help comes from the LORD,
who made heaven and earth! *Psalm 121:1-2*

. . . and then praise God for his deliverance.
Praise the LORD,
who did not let their teeth tear us apart!
We escaped like a bird from a hunter's trap.
The trap is broken, and we are free!
Our help is from the LORD,
who made heaven and earth.   *Psalm 124:6-8*

If we learn anything from the Psalms, it's that God isn't afraid of our emotions, our struggles, and our questions. The one mistake we dare not make, Philip Yancey reminds us, is to confuse *God* (who is good) with *life* (which is hard).[5] God feels the same way we do—and is taking the most radical steps possible (Christmas, Good Friday, Easter, and more to come) to redeem the present situation.

I haven't always believed that. In fact, my father is an atheist. I was raised to *not* believe in God. When I became a Christian, my dad saw it as an act of rebellion. Later, I studied under a German existentialist philosopher. I dared her to prove there isn't a God. "If you're right," I said, in essence, "I'll stop being a Christian." Instead, after studying the writings of the most renowned atheists of the past four centuries, my Christian faith was stronger than ever.

Why is it, I wondered, that these men and women can write brilliantly about any area of philosophy, but they get so angry and irrational when writing about God, the church, and the Christian faith?

After studying their biographies, I discovered the most common reason: Very bad things happened to them or their loved ones, often when they were very young. Many even went on to study in seminary, but they didn't find the answers they were looking for. So they turned against God with a vengeance. It can happen to any of us.

A decade ago I was hit with a rapid-fire series of crises. Emergency surgery for my oldest daughter, who had just been diagnosed with endometriosis, a painful, cancer-like condition. Unexpected house repairs. Two vehicle breakdowns. Huge unpaid bills. I felt that the hand of God was crushing me—emotionally, physically, financially, and in every other way.

How could God do this to my family?

This isn't fair!

My love for God, my joy for life, and my peace were shattered. Instead I felt angry, deceived, and desperate for a way out of my family's nightmare.

In my despair, I doubted God's character. Finally the day came when I couldn't read the Bible anymore. Not a single verse. I couldn't pray, even over a meal. For days and weeks on end.

Experientially, I had lost my faith. Why? Because I had let the circumstances of life temporarily overshadow what I *knew* to be true. As a result, I couldn't fall asleep at night. I couldn't get rid of the stabbing pain in my chest.

Finally, like Peter the apostle at the end of John 6, I realized, "Lord, to whom would we go? You have the words that give eternal life." I dared take the risk of embracing faith again.

Thankfully, God renewed my faith when I started taking several simple (but nonetheless terribly hard) steps of obedience. I forced myself to open my Bible, read a verse—I don't even remember which one—and honestly answer the question, "Do I believe it?" To my surprise, I said yes. It wasn't a big yes. But it was enough to prompt me to read another verse, and then another.

At long last, I felt God speaking to me again. I started praying to him as well. To my surprise, he wasn't angry at me over my crisis of faith. Just the opposite. In time, my faith was renewed in a remarkable way.

Since then, I've talked with many people about my experience.

Not because it's dramatic, but because it's true to life. Every Christian is seriously tempted, at one time or another, to lose his or her faith.

The good news is that God never abandons us. Even in the worst of circumstances, he's still there, urging us not to lose hope that we will see him again.

What's your story? Can you see God at work in your life? If not, let's talk. You can write to me at IfGodDisappears@gmail.com.

OUR WORDS DON'T ALWAYS CONVEY what we really mean.

If a friend tells me he doesn't believe the Bible—that in fact he distrusts it and doesn't want to read it anymore—it sounds as if he hates God's Word. That may be the case. More often, however, what he's really saying—even if he doesn't realize it—is that he's rejecting the distorted, false images of the Bible that he's been exposed to because of a harsh, angry, domineering parent.

If a graduate student tells me she doesn't love God anymore—that in fact she hates God and doesn't want anything to do with him—it sounds as if she hates the God of the Bible, the God who made heaven and earth. That may be the case. More often, however, what she's really saying—even if she doesn't have the wisdom to realize it yet—is that she's rejecting the ugly, even repulsive, images of God that she's been exposed to in some university class.

Satan always repackages that which is intrinsically good—whether it's beauty, sexuality, holiness, justice, or anything else God has created—and makes it repulsive.

It's probably an exaggeration to say most people hate submission.

The fact is, however, the word isn't even in the vocabulary of the average person.

You're free to disagree, but I believe there's nothing the devil would like more than for us to have no idea what it means to submit—in humility—both to God and to a handful of preselected, highly trusted individuals who know and love us.

True submission is built on humility and trust. None of the three are natural for us. Instead, we're mostly good at trying to be self-reliant and are often reckless as a result.

When we embrace humility, however, the transforming power of God's grace begins to be released in and through our lives.

If we come to others in humility, God's grace is poured out through us, making it possible to build relationships of trust.

Of course, we can't trust everybody. But as my friend Paul Goodrich likes to remind me, "Conversely, we can't trust nobody."

Everything good in life requires degrees of well-placed, well-earned trust. We can't simply say, "Trust me." Trust has prerequisites. We all have very active trust processors. When we get hurt by others, our trust meter's sensitivity goes way up. It's easy to end up at the mercy of our trust processor, trusting no one. If that happens, however, we end up forfeiting everything good in life.

Live in isolation long enough and you could develop phenomenal talents and skills. But you can't develop character, integrity, or leadership abilities. Those are developed only within intimate, authentic relationships built on humility, trust, and submission.

Without such relationships, we're rugged individualists bound to lose our faith somewhere along the way.

DAVID'S STORY

Believe me, the word *submit* was nowhere in my vocabulary when I was growing up in the 1960s and 1970s. Like many, I grew up in an antiauthority atmosphere. By the time I was thirteen, my father lectured me on the fact that there were no rules, that I didn't have to obey him anymore, and that I could do whatever I wanted.

Of course, when I made it clear I wanted to become a sold-out follower of Jesus Christ, I made him angry.

But becoming a follower of Jesus Christ didn't automatically mean I understood the transforming power of submission. In fact, like most young men, I had very little idea what it meant to submit.

Three years after I started working at an international communications company, I found myself getting upset about a personnel decision the executive vice president had made. In my mind, he was being a jerk to Susan, one of my colleagues. I couldn't understand why she didn't give that VP a piece of her mind. By the next morning, I was so worked up that I decided—without talking with my wife—to quit my job.

Right before walking out the door at work, I told Susan about my decision. She looked at me and said, "David, that's the dumbest thing I ever heard. First of all, your so-called facts are all wrong. Second, you haven't even thought about lining up another job. Third, have you forgotten you're married and have two kids? If you quit over the approval of *my* job transfer, you're the stupidest person I've ever met."

Okay, Susan didn't exactly call me the stupidest person she'd ever met, but I clearly got the message.

For days afterward, I was shocked. How could I have been so *reckless*?

In the end, the Holy Spirit used Ephesians 5:21 ("Submit to one another") and other Scripture passages to teach me several important, life-changing truths about humility, trust, and submitting to others.

Over time, I grew to understand that submission isn't primarily about power. It's not even primarily about recognizing and following the leadership of those over me, although that's very important. Instead, submission involves actively listening to and heeding the counsel of others. Ultimately, submission based on true humility and authentic, grace-filled relationships of trust is essential among coworkers, friends, and family members.

Whenever I walk away from such relationships and tune out what trusted friends have to say, I'm recklessly messing with my heart and life.

In the end, it could cost me everything.

FAITH WRECKER Living recklessly as a rugged individualist

VINCENT'S STORY

In every sphere of life you'll find story after story about the tragic results that occur when someone has no clue what it means to submit to God, let alone humbly yield to others he or she can trust.

One of the most tragic figures in the art world is Vincent van Gogh. He thought he could have a vertical relationship with God while neglecting or avoiding meaningful relationships with others here on earth. He constantly rebuffed the encouragement, counsel, and advice of his younger brother, Theo, and others who cared about him deeply. Against their urging, Van Gogh left the art world to become a teacher. After he failed at that, he again spurned their advice and tried to become an evangelist.

Unfortunately, this path also seemed to lead him nowhere. Ultimately, Van Gogh's despair brought him to the point of abandoning his faith, thoroughly disappointed with God. He apparently never considered that rather than failing him, God had been trying to speak to him and care for him through those who loved him.

What a difference it would have made if Van Gogh had listened. He could have fulfilled his destiny as an artist to the glory of God. Instead, Van Gogh ended his own life with a bullet.

Why such needless tragedy? Because Van Gogh had no clue what it meant to submit or yield to God, let alone humbly defer to the wisdom and counsel of others he could trust.[1]

PRACTICAL APPLICATIONS

I could tell you story after story about the painful lessons and scars I bear—and wounds I've caused others—because I didn't understand or later lost sight of the value of submitting to God and of deferring to others I can trust.

Early in our marriage, Renée and I tried to handle everything on our own—just the two of us. That plan sometimes met with disaster. After much needless pain, we learned to decide ahead of time to seek the counsel of trusted pastors and elders, respected Christian friends, and a marriage counselor on occasion. Even if things are going well, we have discovered our marriage gets even better if we seek the counsel, advice, encouragement, and support of others.

Or take the issue of health care. When I hit forty, I found myself battling with my primary care physician, who would diagnose a problem, write a prescription, and inform me I had to take a white or orange or green pill every day for the rest of my life. I would take the stupid pill for a few weeks or months until I felt better, stop, end up with all the terrible symptoms again, and then go back to Dr. Wells, only to be told, "David, you *have* to take this pill every day for the rest of your life."

Until I settled the issue of submission to my primary care physician, I was miserable. It took a while, but finally common sense prevailed. I needed to humble myself, trust my doctor, and yield to his wisdom and expertise. As soon as I submitted—*ta-da!*—I felt a whole lot better.

Then there's the matter of unexpected crises. Of course, one hopes that life's crises will be few and far between. But several months ago we found ourselves in back-to-back crises. First, I contracted an acute form of bronchitis. Renée had to rush me to urgent care, where they put me on oxygen. When my fingers kept turning blue, the physician on duty called an ambulance to rush me to a nearby hospital. Within a few hours, I still felt absolutely wiped out, but I was able to return home with an inhaler and two prescription drugs in hand.

Unfortunately, during the initial evaluation when the ER staff asked me what prescription drugs I took, I forgot one. Worse, I didn't double-check with my primary care physician before I started taking the two new drugs. A severe drug reaction just about put me back in the hospital. If I were single, I would have been admitted. Instead, Renée agreed to take care of me around the clock. I was too weak to do anything.

Finally, Renée and I both realized we needed to ask for prayer. We left a voice mail message for our church's senior pastor. I must have sounded pretty bad, because less than an hour later, the pastor and the chairman of our elder board were knocking on my front door. They came in, listened to my story, and then prayed earnestly for my healing. Within hours I was back on my feet, and within three days was almost completely recovered.

Would I have gotten better if I hadn't asked a couple of elders to pray for me? Probably, but my doctor had predicted that could take three to six *weeks*. Besides, I was so wiped out I knew I needed their encouragement and prayers.

Why do I tell that story? Because the reality is, we're all going to experience the crises of life, usually when we least expect them, often from a completely unexpected source. Before those crises hit, we have a decision to make.

Are we going to handle life as rugged individualists?

Or are we going to deliberately and proactively respond in humility, trust, and submission? When I was sick, I probably should have contacted my church much sooner than I did. Again, submission isn't a natural part of my DNA. Truth be told, I'm a rugged individualist through and through. But by God's grace, I'm learning a better way.

Some years ago, I made a pact with a small group of fellow Christian brothers, men I could trust. We agreed to be there for each other through thick and thin. I've also given them complete permission to speak to me about my life, addressing weaknesses and pointing out blind spots. These men help me to stay focused on God rather than my own wants and desires.

Why doesn't individualism work? Or to put it another way, why is submission so important? After fifteen years of lay pastoral ministry, I've seen just about everything. Whenever I'm counseling someone, I try to ascertain as quickly as possible whether or not the individual has deliberately, consciously, willingly submitted to Christlike individuals who can be trusted. If so, there's hope. No matter how bleak the circumstances, God can always heal, restore, and renew the brokenhearted.

Ultimately, when it comes to submission based on trust and humility, or any other aspect of life and godliness, we see the perfect model within the Trinity—God the Father, God the Son, and God the Holy Spirit. In the Trinity, there are different functional roles in the midst of complete equality, harmony, and intimacy. We never have to worry about the Father dominating the Son, or a power struggle breaking out between the Son and the Spirit. Instead, they're one.

Wise men and women throughout history have taught that a right view of God in heaven will save us from ten thousand ills here on earth. That's certainly true when it comes to submission through humility and trust.

Even the wisest and best, however, still wrestle with the need to yield to others. Suddenly, the refreshing atmosphere of love and grace disappears. Sharp words are exchanged. Division occurs. Just look at Paul and Barnabas in the book of Acts. They were the closest of friends for years. Then, after several heated arguments, they chose to go their separate ways. But of course that conflict wasn't the end of the story. Later they reconciled and were closer than ever. So please don't close this book and walk away discouraged if submission is hard for you.

DEBUNKING MYTHS

Let's look at what the Bible says—and doesn't say—about submitting.

Ephesians 5:21 says, "Submit to one another out of reverence for Christ."

I believe this passage needs to be understood in the broader context, which—leading up to this verse—builds a strong case for true, Christlike humility and for authentic relationships of trust. Only then can the paragraphs that follow, in which Paul talks about submission within marriage, family, employment, and life's toughest trials and tribulations, make any sense.

Before we go any further, I want to clearly state three important truths about submission and clear up several misconceptions.

First, submission isn't possible unless someone knowingly, deliberately, and decisively rejects the American ideal of rugged individualism. Unless I reject that mentality, I'll know nothing of submitting to others' strengths—and I'll pay a dear price.

Second, while Scripture commands us to submit to one another, it doesn't give us the authority to command others to submit to us. That would be as ludicrous as commanding someone to love or respect us. Submission must be earned. It builds upon the positive aspects of true humility and grace-filled trust. Only when those two things are in place is healthy, Christlike submission even possible.

Third, submission doesn't mean taking orders. Instead, it means being *willing* to yield or defer to the strengths of others. This is true not only in marriage but in every sphere of life, including a relationship with God.

Submitting to God and others isn't easy in the best of times let alone in the worst. Just ask Kim and Michelle.

Cultivating relationships of humility, trust, and submission

FAITH BUILDER

KIM'S STORY

For more than a decade, Kim Dilworth was an aspiring young television news reporter on a mission to get to the top. She went from station to station, state to state, and finally landed a job at one of the largest television stations in the United States.

All this time God was whispering in her ear, *Kim, come home. You've forgotten what's most important in your life.* But Kim had her own ideas about success and what she needed to do to get there. So rather than trusting that God might have a better plan for her life, or returning to the Christian faith she had heard about in church as a child, she ignored his gentle promptings in her rush to get the next breaking story.

Then came the unexpected. "Kim," the news director said, "we aren't going to renew your contract."

No reason, no explanation, no joke! In one minute she went from being a recognized television personality to being an unemployed single woman.

Embarrassed and confused, Kim went to the only place she could think of to hide: the woods. She stomped through miles of trail. Along the way, an old tree stump caught Kim's attention. Someone with a big chain saw had reduced a beautiful oak tree to ruins. *It's just like my life,* Kim thought, *destroyed in minutes.*

"Please, God, give me back my life!" she pleaded.

It seemed that God was listening, and Kim got another job as a freelance reporter right away. "Thank you, God!" she exclaimed, thinking that this was her miracle. As she covered her new beat, she began noticing billboards, bus boards, and yard signs all over town advertising a big music festival with a message. She didn't want to miss it.

She listened as the speaker delivered a simple message: "We are all like sheep, each gone our own way. But God laid on Jesus the sins of us all." Kim had heard those words a hundred times and always considered herself to be a Christian.

"But truth be told," she said to me later, "I had never fully surrendered to God. I decided it was time I did."

After the festival, Kim joined a local church, was baptized, and went to work for a ministry helping the urban poor.

A couple of years later, Kim went on a hike and found herself back at that old stump. To her surprise, a strong, young sapling had sprouted out of the ruins and was growing straight toward the sky.

"What God did for that old stump, he did tenfold in my life," Kim says. In place of her rugged individualism, Kim now surrenders her choices and plans to God, come what may.

Sadly, not everyone's story is marked by such profound rebirth. The choices of individuals we trust early in life can rip our lives apart like a hurricane. Without our even realizing it, havoc can lead us to embrace anything but healthy relationships with God and others.

MICHELLE'S STORY

Michelle's parents divorced when she was only eighteen months old. Her father remarried, moved to another state, and took only minimal interest in Michelle and her brother. Mostly, their contact with him involved his annual excursion to his parents' house in Dubuque, Iowa, when Michelle and her brother were always sent to play while their father chatted with his parents.

Michelle's mother remarried a couple of years after the divorce. Stepfather number one had a drinking problem and lost the rent money more than once. That marriage lasted six years.

A short time later, stepfather number two came into the picture and completely ruined what little good Michelle and her brother and mother had known. As a con artist, he took their trust and betrayed them. Less than fifteen months after he came into their lives, he was convicted on rape and sodomy charges in another state and sent to prison.

Michelle was afraid to say anything to her mother about what had been happening until the first prison visit. "I was scared, angry, and repulsed at what I saw there in the visiting room, and tired of pretending that I cared at all about this monster," Michelle says. After she and her mother and brother talked, denial was impossible: This man had emotionally, physically, and sexually abused all three of them. Michelle's mother immediately filed for divorce, but the damage had been done.

Within a year, the family started attending church. Michelle made a profession of faith and was baptized at age twelve. But just before her twenty-first birthday, Michelle decided to "leave God and make my own way in the world." So off she went, to one bad choice after another. Her choices eventually led to an eight-year affair with an older man who took advantage of his position of power.

Years later, Michelle has come back to God, but not without a struggle. The issue for her, as it is for most of us, was a five-letter word. In her own words:

> Pride is equal to saying, "I can do this all myself, thank you very much. I have my best interests in mind." I believe that this emotion is the opposite of trust.

> Trust is exhibited best when we are completely incapable of providing something for ourselves—and believe that God has our best interests at heart. To "wait on the Lord" shows not only patience, but trust. Belief. Faith.

> Trust broken at an early age, or any age, for that matter, is difficult to replace. When personal boundaries are violated by someone who was trusted to act with our best interests in mind, building trust again is very difficult. Trust in people. Trust in God. I'm still learning.

What's remarkable to me is that Michelle doesn't blame others for her choice to walk away from God. Instead, she points to her own pride.

Pride is the one word the devil wants to dress up as if it means something beautiful. Today we almost never hear it spoken of as one of the seven deadly sins, so I deliberately left it out of the title of this chapter. Until the end of this chapter, I didn't use the word. Yet in the end, Michelle convinced me that I had to mention it by name. Frankly, her honest appraisal caught me off guard.

It's one thing to admit that I'm a rugged individualist. It's another to admit my pride, yet in the end I must. We all must.

Otherwise, as Michelle and I can attest, we'll live recklessly and inevitably fall.

Otherwise, true humility, trust, and submission are impossible.

Otherwise, not only does God disappear, we do as well. In the end, it's our pride that must fall.

WHEN WE TELL OUR KIDS SOMETHING, Renée and I usually find they'll *eventually* do what we say. But the initial reaction is, "I'm not sure I just heard that" or "I'm not quite ready to do what you just said."

Our kids are smart. They've learned that displaying outright, high-handed rebellion in front of their parents often produces some rather immediate and unpleasant consequences.

But Renée and I have become increasingly aware that our children are masters at cunningly and often quietly disobeying us—at least initially. It's amazing how good they are at this.

I knock on Benjamin's bedroom door a few minutes before dinner, look him in the eye, smile, and ask him to pick up his toys.

Ben looks at the new army green wristwatch he got for Christmas and acknowledges that he needs to have all the toys picked up by 6:05 p.m. I pat myself on the back for giving him that watch and go downstairs to let his sister Anna know that dinner is about to be served.

When I come back upstairs, however, there's Ben, with twice as many toys scattered all over his bedroom floor as there were a couple of minutes earlier, and a blank look when I ask him why.

Or Renée asks Anna to do something. Anna might immediately go off to do what she's been asked, but as she does, her lower lip is drooping and her steps are heavy. It's obvious that she'd rather *not* do what Mom just asked.

And when I ask Anna to do something, she looks at me like I must be off my rocker: "But, Dad, don't you know Mom already asked me to do this other thing?" Most of the time, I have to admit I *didn't* know that. But, between you and me, I also wonder why doing that other chore suddenly became so important when she was so reluctant to do it only a few seconds earlier.

How thoughtful of God to give me children who remind me of my own capacity to put his commands on "pause" at times. To paraphrase the words of the prophet Isaiah, "We like children have gone astray, each of us putting off obeying God in our own little way."

THE LITTLE STUFF

Let's face it. Benjamin doesn't want to live by my rules because at his age, he's ruled by his own wants and desires. For him, "Have fun" is a rule, and it takes priority over my rule to "Clean up and come eat." Anna follows the rules, but in her heart, she still tightly grips her own set of rules. Both illustrate how I sometimes behave with God—or despite him.

Granted, most of us don't wake up in the morning and say, "I think I'm going to deliberately rebel against God and mess up my life today."

No, we much more often choose to sin by small degrees.

How prone we are to hear God's Word and then shortly after ponder, "Well, I am forgiven, after all, and I'm not quite strong enough to obey that anyway."

The problem, as the book of James reminds us, is that to disobey God in one little point is tantamount to rebelling against everything God has said.

Little sins eventually betray a serious defect deep in our hearts.

By "little," of course, I mean little in our eyes, not in God's eyes. Sin is sin.

That I am quite glad not to murder anyone today is no great virtue when I'm ignoring God's presence in my life.

When I look back at all the sins I've committed along the way the past few weeks, I get worried.

What's wrong with me? Or, perhaps better put, why am I so self-inclined and so God-averse? Why am I so apt to choose my will, my way, my timing, instead of choosing God's will, God's way, God's timing?

I act as if God's rules—any rules—are bad. Of course, they're often good. I saw this demonstrated at my son Benjamin's first basketball practice last season. With clearly defined rules enforced by the coaches and referees, the boys can have a lot of fun. Without rules, however, the game quickly turns ugly, and boys end up getting hurt. It's anything but entertaining, enjoyable, or fun.

The same is true in every sphere of life—sports, education, music, family, church, employment, transportation, technology—you name it. In many cases, rules are essential.

Rules can protect us and help us predict the behavior of those around us. If they aren't autocratically made, changed, or enforced, rules can be very good—or at the very least, ethically neutral—for our society. If you've ever visited a major city in a developing country, you've no doubt seen the traffic congestion at every major intersection and realized the importance of traffic lights and the rules that require us to obey them.

Of course, sometimes we need to break the rules to maintain a higher ideal, which happens every time an ambulance turns on its siren and goes through a red light.

We always need to keep things in perspective: God is far greater than any rules. Focus too much on the rules, especially rules of our own making or reshaping, and we miss God's heart and very presence in our midst.

FAITH WRECKER   Making our own rules, whatever the cost

MEET THE BRUTE SQUAD

In Matthew 15 and Mark 7, we find Jesus surrounded by Pharisees and scribes, the religious leaders of his day. They were a brute squad, looking for a reason to attack Jesus. At lunchtime, they found it: The followers of Jesus broke one of the Pharisees' petty rules about ceremonial hand washing.

The focus of the Pharisees and scribes was entirely on looking good externally—and smacking anyone who wasn't zealous enough to comply with all their traditions, customs, and manmade rules. You can almost picture the switches in their hands, whacking people left and right. The ridiculous thing here, of course, is that they were lifting their switches to strike God himself. This brute squad wasn't reacting impulsively. Instead, they were premeditative and calculating.

So the Pharisees picked a fight with Jesus. Their reason for getting so upset, however, is a bit foreign to most of us.

Ceremonial hand washing certainly isn't unique to the Jewish people in Bible times; it's been practiced by many non-Jewish people groups for thousands of years. I saw this firsthand when I was visiting my friends Larry and Dianne Burke, who live among the Dangaleat people in north central Africa. Many Dangaleat have been transplanted in recent years to the slums of N'Djamena, the capital of Chad. Most of them, however, still live in the interior in a region they call the Guera—a vast, sparsely populated sub-Saharan wasteland hundreds of miles to the east of the city.

To visit N'Djamena is shocking enough. To travel into the interior is to leave everything you've ever known, cross an invisible boundary, and then step into a surreal, completely undeveloped, mostly duotone world that's difficult to take in, let alone describe.

The desert goes on and on for hundreds of miles. Looking for a green tree under which to rest in the shade is almost futile. When you do find a tree, it's often twenty feet tall and bristling with two-inch thorns that threaten to pierce your feet and clothing at every angle. Even the brush in the area is surreal. One common bush has large objects hanging off of it that look like green water balloons ready to burst. Inside those playful-looking "balloons," however, is a terrible poison that will burn your skin like acid.

The Dangaleat people live in fourteen villages scattered over roughly a hundred miles of the Guera. They are subsistence farmers. Their methods of raising crops in the sub-Saharan desert are ingenious. Yet drought and pestilence are constant threats.

In most parts of Chad, water is at a high premium. Clean water is almost unknown. Still, before every meal, where eating with the hands is customary, I was required to go through a ritual hand-washing ceremony. Of course, I bucked against the idea of pouring contaminated water on my relatively clean hands. Still, it had to be done. I've never prayed so hard before eating. *God save me from getting sick!*

In Old Testament times, God's laws required only the priests, at certain times, to perform hand-washing ceremonies. It wasn't until later, after the rise of the Pharisees following the Babylonian captivity, that this very specific requirement stretched beyond anything God intended.

Ironically, the Pharisees couldn't see the hypocrisy of their mixed-up morality. They were making false accusations of sin, which is far worse than not washing your hands before you eat. These religious leaders were educated beyond the obvious; they were absolutely blind to what is truly right and wrong.

Of course, many believe the most important commands are the ones God gives. Even then, not all commands are created equal. Some commands are perpetual, for all people for all time. Other commands have clearly expired, and still others are for someone else—not for you and me.

Jesus said he didn't come to earth to abolish the Old Testament Law; instead, he came to fulfill it. That point was lost on the Pharisees, who were out of touch with reality and adamant in their denial of Jesus' person, power, and authority. They wanted Jesus to obey their rules, whereas Jesus insisted he was the one who gave the Ten Commandments and inspired the rest of the Old Testament. If Jesus is to be believed, he is the one who calls the shots—not the Pharisees or scribes, and certainly not you or me.

So Jesus rebuked these hypocritical religious leaders. Jesus then went on to prove that this brute squad was systematically breaking God's law left and right. Jesus quoted one of the Ten Commandments: "Honor your father and mother."

The Pharisees had twisted this command 180 degrees in the wrong direction. They taught people to use the word *corban*, which referred to when a person dedicated something or everything they owned to God. Corban is good if used as God instructed, but the Pharisees were using it as a way to shirk any responsibility of caring for their elderly or disabled parents. A son could simply say the magic word without ever really giving any of his money or possessions to God. *Ta-da! I'm not obligated to honor my parents, no matter what the Lord says.*

Over the years, the Pharisees and scribes had made up many such rules to circumvent the letter and spirit of God's recorded words. In the same way, whenever my "rules" contradict God's clear-cut statements, I'm choosing to reject him.

The Pharisees and scribes were speaking angry, murderous words against Jesus in public. This shocked the disciples, but it didn't shock Jesus. Jesus knew exactly what they were thinking, so it's no wonder that he told his disciples to stay away from the Pharisees. This command applies to us, as well. Jesus wants us to stay away from anyone who pretends to speak for God and yet openly and directly opposes what he says.

Then Jesus taught his disciples about the real source of all the evil—the evil we hear about on the news day in and day out. The list of evils isn't exhaustive, of course. Jesus could have just as easily added other sins he and Moses and Isaiah and Peter and Paul warned against. Interestingly, Matthew 15 lists seven such evils. Mark 7 lists thirteen. The two overlapping lists cover just about all of the Ten Commandments. Of course, the book of James tells us that anytime I choose my will over against God's revealed will, I'm breaking the whole law.

The reality is that all the Ten Commandments have been broken by all people in all cultures for all time. Where do these sins come from? Jesus makes it clear: They come from inside, in our hearts.

A thousand years earlier, in the book of Proverbs, wise King Solomon warned us to guard our hearts (Proverbs 4:23). If we don't guard our hearts, evil things will come out. This applies to every sphere of life, and it certainly proved true in Solomon's own experience.

Whatever we do, let's not kid ourselves about the source of evil.

IF THERE IS NO GOD

In my book with Luis Palau *God Is Relevant,* I noted that when Dostoevsky wrote the line, "If there is no God, everything is permitted," in all likelihood he meant more than "I can do whatever I want." Rabbi Harold Kushner says, "I suspect he means 'Without

God, what makes something I do wrong? It may be illegal. It may be distasteful to you. It may hurt people who don't deserve to be hurt. But if I feel good doing it, what makes it *wrong*?'"[1]

Indeed, without a divine point of reference, who's to say what's right and wrong?

We see this in the sexual affairs of Arthur Schopenhauer, Karl Marx, Friedrich Nietzsche, Sigmund Freud, John-Paul Sartre, Aldous Huxley, Bertrand Russell, and even Albert Einstein, all of whom resisted classic Judeo-Christian ethics.

Russell called Christianity "the principal enemy of moral progress [including sexual liberation] in the world."[2] It's important to remember that Russell wasn't saying this for purely intellectual reasons. If I want to discard God's rules, there's a reason why.

In *Ends and Means*, Huxley admitted, "I had motives for not wanting the world to have a meaning; consequently assumed that it had none, and was able without any difficulty to find satisfying reasons for this assumption. Most ignorance is vincible ignorance. We don't know because we don't want to know."[3]

When Charles Darwin was asked whether man was in any way unique from other life-forms, he is reported to have replied, "Of all expressions, blushing seems to be the most strictly human." Mark Twain later quipped, "Man is the only animal that blushes. Or needs to."[4] No matter how hard we try to reject standards of right and wrong, we all have them. Even if they're skewed and sometimes don't make sense.

Media giant and self-described agnostic Ted Turner once remarked, rather sternly, that "If you're not perfect, you shouldn't tell other people what to do."[5]

Shouldn't?

Unless we have a basis on which to say what's right and wrong, it doesn't work to try to make value statements. Some basis is essential.

Even atheist J. L. Mackie suggested, "Moral properties constitute so odd a cluster of qualities and relations that they are most unlikely to have arisen in the ordinary course of events without an all-powerful god to create them."[6]

Fellow atheist Kai Nielsen points out, "The sense of moral relativism, skepticism and nihilism rampant in our age is due in large measure to the general weakening of religious belief in an age of science. Without God there can be no objective foundation for our moral beliefs. . . . Without religious belief, without the Living God, there could be no adequate answer to the persistently gnawing questions: What ought we to do? How ought I to live?"[7]

Of course, it's impossible to live without rules. So, most of us are pretty good at making up our own rules despite the truth and regardless of the consequences. Ravi Zacharias says, "Any antitheist who lives a moral life merely lives *better* than his or her philosophy warrants."[8]

Conversely, it's possible to twist God's rules like the brute squad in Jesus' day. Rabbi Kushner writes, "I have to admit that some of my best friends are atheists. They never darken the doorway of either church or synagogue," yet they are good people, while some regular synagogue or church members are "small-souled people, insecure and judgmental, quick to find fault with others."[9] I would certainly agree.[10]

No wonder Jesus warned his listeners to stay away from anyone who claimed to speak for God and yet was angry with God or put his own rules or teachings—or anyone else's rules or teachings— above God's Word.

You may be single, married, separated, divorced, or widowed. You may be straight, gay, bisexual, or transgender. You may be in your teens, twenties, thirties, or forties. You may be in your fifties, sixties, seventies, or older. You may have had a good life so far, may have had your share of ups and downs, or may have gone through some pretty devastating experiences. Wherever you're at in life, I believe Jesus has something to say to all of us.

When people heard the news about the Ted Haggard scandal, many people asked, "How could he?" The reality is, if you and I don't courageously make choices based on God's truth (instead of making our own rules), someday people may ask the same question about us. This tragic result is true to Scripture, true to church history, and true to contemporary biography.

When it's all said and done, we need to submit to those in leadership over us (in any sphere of life) as long as their rules don't force us to disobey God or violate our values. We need to stubbornly resist the temptation to start making our own rules or start bending the rules of others to our own advantage. We also need to do our best to avoid twisting God's rules, commands, and teachings found or affirmed in the New Testament.

Sometimes, though, we need to break one rule in order to reach or retain a higher ideal.

FAITH BUILDER   **Being courageous enough to make choices based on the truth**

BREAKING THE RULES

The last time I had to fly out of Los Angeles, I was stuck in a traffic jam and arrived at my gate with only a half hour until my plane boarded. What a relief! Until a single mom and her three-year-old sat down next to me. The little girl was crying inconsolably. Nothing the woman said or did stifled her daughter's loud sobs.

In exasperation, an airline employee walked over with a huge candy bar and offered it to the girl. More crying.

I know strangers (who aren't in uniform) aren't supposed to talk to little girls. But sometimes a rule has to be broken. So I pulled out my cell phone, popped it open, clicked on photos, and turned to my left.

"Hey, do you want to see a silly picture of my little girl?" I asked. I showed her a photo of Anna waving her arms and smiling.

The crying subsided a bit.

"Hey, here's another silly picture—of my youngest son." I showed her a closeup shot of Benjamin pretending to eat my cell phone.

The crying stopped.

I kept showing her goofy pictures of everyone in my family in a desperate bid to keep the little girl quiet.

It worked. After mothers with small children boarded my flight, businessmen started heading over to where I was sitting. One slapped me on the back, smiling, and said, "Good job!"

Hey, even small-time heroes need to break the rules every once in a while, right?

After all, not all rules are good. I've come to believe that rules can be morally bad when they contradict or oppose what's true.

By "true," I'm speaking of what God has said in Scripture ("love one another" and care for "the least of these") over what mere mortals have to say ("children shouldn't talk to strangers" and "strangers shouldn't talk to children").

Truth is the standard by which everything should be judged, including what I say in this chapter. As with all of life, you should question anything that appears to contradict truth.

That often takes a lot of courage.

GAINING COURAGE

A mentor once told me that we sense God's presence most when we're most alive. By "alive," he meant when we're out in nature, when we put ourselves at risk, or when we find ourselves in a crisis.

Imminent danger—real or perceived—triggers the strongest of human emotions. Fear is hardwired into our minds. Without thinking, we are prompted to shut up, freeze up, even give up. The good news: We can rewire our thoughts, beliefs, and automatic responses.

Life is full of circumstances that test our courage. Winston Churchill once said, "Without courage, all other virtues lose their meaning." It doesn't matter that you're honest, for instance, if you're reluctant to embrace God's truth. Or that you're responsible if you're afraid to ask God for wisdom, strength, and joy.

I see myself as a fairly courageous person. The hard part for me is separating courage from recklessly breaking or bending life's most important rules.

As a young man, I loved to hike through the Cascades and Olympic Mountains in western Washington state. Twice my father, brother, and I hiked to Glacier Peak and then traversed up its sides.

During our second trip, we decided to go up the mountain's largest glacier, a steep 12,500-foot diagonal climb, digging out every handhold and foothold for twelve straight hours until we reached the top of the glacier (only a few hours from the summit).

We had been staring at hardpacked snow and ice all day without a break to rest, let alone eat. Suddenly, we could look out over the Cascade mountain range. It was breathtaking.

Then came the urgent work of staking our tents as securely as possible before howling winds hit with hurricane force. Anything that wasn't secure blew away. Half the night I thought that might be our fate as well.

Morning dawned with a strange quietness. Long before sunrise, a huge cloud cover had swept over the north Cascades. Besides the top of Glacier Peak above us, the only things we could see were four other mountain peaks in the far distance. Worse, we quickly realized, the clouds were rising. All plans to reach the summit before lunch were abandoned. Instead, we broke camp and prepared for a rapid descent.

Given the extremely steep slope in front of us, I proposed that we glissade down the glacier. (Picture stepping off a ledge and dropping feet first at thirty to forty miles an hour while skiing on your boots.)

It would be impossible to fall backward, I argued.

What I should have added: Avoid rolling forward at all costs. And watch out for truck-sized rocks near the bottom of the glacier.

What took us twelve hours to climb up took us less than five minutes to descend. We dropped 4,650 feet in elevation. It was the adrenaline ride of a lifetime.

Afterward, I realized that one false move while glissading would have meant almost instant death.

So much for making my own rules whatever the cost.

It's ironic that our society is bent on the idea of trying to become more rebellious, less principled, more risk taking, less inhibited, more outrageous, less self-controlled. Many blame these trends on the 1960s, but the reality is people have always had a natural bent against making wise choices based on truth.

I did some pretty stupid things as a young man. None of those actions, including glissading, were motivated by God. It's only by his grace that I lived long enough to get married.

Granted, you may have an ocean of pain and a sea of questions, few of which will likely be healed or answered in this life, but I implore you to consider this: Throughout Scripture, the first and foremost theme is God's heart to reconcile individuals to himself. Someday our bodies will fall apart. No amount of vitamins or exercise or medicine or surgery or replacement parts can prevent that from happening. But the Bible says our souls live forever—

something we would be wise to keep mindful of along our journey. That's why Scripture says repeatedly that God doesn't want anyone to perish.

To perish means to miss out on the life God intended for us to enjoy. The last message of Peter is worth considering. What was utmost on his mind? First, we take God at his word, cling to it, believe what he has said, and refuse to be carried away by false teaching. Second, we are commanded to live pure lives, keeping our eyes on eternity—not on what is temporal and soon to fade away. And third, and this is my point here, Peter reminded us that God is "being patient . . . He does not want anyone to be destroyed."

God's desire that we truly live, however, doesn't happen easily.

BEYOND COURAGE

For the most part, I see myself as a fairly courageous person. From time to time, however, I've fought periodic episodes of deep discouragement. We all have. It comes with the territory on this fallen planet we're sometimes tempted to call home.

God revolutionized my thinking while I was studying the life of Elijah in 1 Kings 17–19.

In my reading of Scripture, I can find no other biblical character (besides Jesus) who showed more courage than Elijah. After the glory days of King Solomon, God raised up Elijah to confront the immense wickedness, gross idolatry, and rampant paganism that consumed Israel.

The first lesson we learn from the life of Elijah is that God honors the courage of his people.

But before we get to that, let's set the scene. Ahab has taken the throne as the eighth king of Israel (after the kingdom's split). More vile than anyone before him, Ahab is married to Jezebel, a Sidonian whose chief ambition in life is to propagate a gross form of paganism in Israel and utterly destroy all worship of the true God. She has murdered many of God's prophets, priests, and teachers. I believe if anyone ever was inspired by Satan himself, it was this woman—and her equally wicked husband, King Ahab.

It's onto this stage that Elijah steps, pronouncing God's judgment on Israel and declaring that God is shutting the heavens. "As surely as the LORD, the God of Israel, lives—the God I serve—there will be no dew or rain during the next few years until I give the word!" Imagine the audacity it took to say something like that! It's ludicrous—unless God told him to say it.

Because Elijah understood the difference between following human rules and following God's rules, he was courageous enough to take God at his word, confront Ahab, and pronounce such a judgment in the name of the one true God of heaven and earth.

After pronouncing this judgment on the wicked nation of Israel, Elijah heads east across the Jordan River to live in the wilderness along a brook in the Kerith Ravine, near his hometown of Tishbe.

When the brook dries up, God commands Elijah to go to a coastal town in Sidon practically next door to wicked Queen Jezebel's hometown. And again, Elijah shows courage by obeying God. God's protection is clear as the Scripture tells us that King Ahab "searched every nation and kingdom on earth from end to end" but still couldn't find him!

Time passes, and God's judgment on Israel reduces the once prosperous nation to poverty. It hasn't rained in three and a half years, and Ahab is absolutely desperate—although he still stubbornly refuses to acknowledge that he is the reason for the terrible famine that has stricken the entire land. And he utterly refuses to turn away from his idolatrous lifestyle.

Now that Ahab has clearly demonstrated his rebellion against

God, the Lord tells Elijah to go back and confront him once again. This would have been the equivalent, at the height of the Persian Gulf War, of someone flying to the Middle East, sneaking into Iraq, and pronouncing the God of Israel's judgment on Saddam Hussein.

But Elijah goes, announcing his arrival to King Ahab's chief of staff. When Ahab sees the prophet, the king's immediate response is to cry out, "So, is it really you, you troublemaker of Israel?"

After Elijah's showdown with the prophets of Baal, God honors his courage by sending lightning from heaven to devour the evening sacrifice. Elijah becomes an instant national hero, as he orders the death of Baal's prophets and announces the onset of a "mighty rainstorm."

Ahab prepares to head for home, but the Scriptures tell us that "the LORD gave special strength to Elijah. He tucked his cloak into his belt and ran ahead of Ahab's chariot all the way to the entrance of Jezreel."

What's the importance of Elijah racing ahead of the king? If he had been following human rules, Elijah would have simply figured that the king deserved what was coming to him (God's wrath), but because he followed God's rules, the prophet knew he needed to give Ahab one more chance to turn from his sin. It took great courage to do what Elijah did.

A few hours later, however, we find Ahab arriving back at his palace, dripping wet and covered with mud. Jezebel is furious. The Sidonian's schemes have failed: Her imported prophets of Baal and Asherah have been put to death. She doesn't take this lightly and vows to kill the prophet Elijah before another day goes by.

It's here that Elijah proves he's human just like us. If you've ever found yourself too tired and stressed to obey God anymore, you probably can understand what Elijah does next. In a moment of physical weakness (he's just run more than fifteen miles back to the city, remember!), Elijah becomes emotionally distraught over Jezebel's murderous threats. His courage is lagging. Instead of crying out to God in prayer and seeking his will, Elijah panics, goes into spiritual neutral, and hightails it south into the desert of Beersheba. In his utter panic, Elijah leaves his servant behind in the town and flees into the wilderness to save his own skin.

- Physically, Elijah becomes further exhausted.
- Emotionally, he's completely devastated.
- Spiritually, he's out of touch with God.
- Socially, he's utterly isolated.

It isn't until Elijah collapses under a desert tree in abject despair that he finally remembers to pray. And what a prayer it is! "I have had enough, LORD. . . . Take my life." His courage is completely gone.

Vince Lombardi, coach of the Super Bowl champion Green Bay Packers, once remarked, "Fatigue makes cowards of us all." If ever there was a coward, it was Elijah out there in the desert of Beersheba. What's a prophet of God doing in a place like that?

The truth is, we're no different than Elijah. We share the same DNA. There are times when even the best of us prove to be cowards. We're most vulnerable whenever we're

- physically exhausted
- emotionally upset
- spiritually dry
- socially isolated

Think about it. What do you do when the storms of life hit? Immediately pick up the phone and ask someone to pray for you? Open God's Word and ask him to speak to you? Listen to music to encourage your heart? And get a good night's sleep? Or are you like Elijah? "Woe is me. It doesn't get any worse than this. Just let me die, Lord. I've had enough."

Often it's during times of physical, emotional, spiritual, and social stress that we're most tempted to turn from God's laws and live by our own. (Elijah did this by running to the desert in fear—the law of self-protection.) But when we do, we inevitably find ourselves further from God than when we started. And it seems as if God disappears.

It's critical that we see how God responds to Elijah at his moment of greatest discouragement and despair. Does God strike him dead? No. He ministers to Elijah, cares for him, and puts him back on his feet.

- Physically, God provides much needed food and rest.
- Emotionally, God allows Elijah to sense his presence.
- Spiritually, God exhorts Elijah to follow him again.
- Socially, God urges Elijah to remember seven thousand other God followers who haven't been killed by Jezebel yet.

Back on his feet, Elijah heads north out of the desert of Beersheba and onto the pages of Scripture as one of the greatest heroes of the faith.

Because Elijah was human just like us, we can learn a great lesson from his response to a crisis when God seemed to disappear. Instead of running away, we need to turn to God, trusting that he will respond and meet our needs.

Just as he cared for Elijah, God promises to care for you and me—we need only to call out his name and ask.

Whatever we do, let's not start making our own rules, whatever the cost.

No matter what happens, let's be courageous enough to make choices based on the truth.

DURING OUR COURTSHIP, Renée and I often enjoyed out-ings along picturesque Lake Washington near Seattle. Once we even borrowed a boat and spent a romantic afternoon sailing around the lake together.

Shortly before our anniversary a decade later, I took Renée sailing again. I was envisioning a romantic, carefree afternoon. Any such dreams were quickly dashed, however, when strong winds spun the ten-foot sailboat around and around toward the south end of the lake. Renée and I furiously attempted to adjust the sails and maneuver the rudder to get us back on course.

We both lost our tempers in a hurry. Only after reaching the far shore did we discover a problem with the rudder. Not that that made Renée any happier with me!

Sadly, that's only one of countless occasions when a loved one and I have lost our tempers and hurt each other's feelings.

It's not coincidental that people who use profanity do so when they're angry. I can't be filled with rage at anyone without also feeling rage toward God.

HATE MAIL

Tragically, the world is full of hate—hate voice mail, hate songs, hate movies, hate blogs, hate e-mail, and good old-fashioned hate letters.

Just ask the editors at any daily newspaper in America.

Over the past two decades, a handful of religious leaders have helped change the face of the American mainstream media for *good*. But almost nobody talks about those changes.

Sadly, most Christians don't know anyone in the media, and many refuse to give them the benefit of the doubt. Rather than looking at the positive influence that media can have on spirituality, many focus on the liberal reporting and secular biases of some journalists, claiming that the media as a whole is the greatest enemy of religion ever. The results of this belief can be disastrous. Consider the following example.

At the urging of Billy Graham, the Portland *Oregonian* newspaper hired a full-time religion writer named Mark O'Keefe, gave him a great deal of freedom to cover the religious side of news stories, and often featured his articles on page one.

A religion reporter's dream job? Hardly.

O'Keefe started receiving scores of hate voice mail messages and hate letters via post, fax, and e-mail from so-called Christians who had no idea that O'Keefe was actually a follower of Jesus Christ. Many of these zealots were so focused on their anger against non-Christians that they completely missed the point of his in-depth articles.

After O'Keefe moved to Washington, D.C., to work as a national correspondent for the Newhouse News Service, the *Oregonian* hired another religion writer. Tragically, she has received the same volume of hate messages once directed toward O'Keefe. Thankfully, a handful of Christians have befriended her and made it clear that the hateful minority doesn't speak for Jesus Christ or his followers.

Like any author worth his or her salt, I've also stirred up a lot of anger . . .

. . . when my wife and I did an immense amount of research in the early 1980s and then wrote an extensive piece for *The Other Side* (an alternative Christian magazine) in favor of in vitro fertilization (within specific ethical guidelines), to the consternation of everyone from Jerry Falwell to the pope.

. . . when I did more research and wrote against the age-old hypothesis that Proverbs 31:10-31 was written for women (it sounds sexist, but almost all the evidence shows it was written for men: *Do you want a wife like this? Then do these things*).

. . . when I did nine more months of research and coauthored Doubleday's critically acclaimed book *God Is Relevant* in 1997 (the first evangelistic book published by a leading New York publisher since *Mere Christianity* by C. S. Lewis).

. . . when I helped Brian McLaren, Dan Kimball, Spencer Burke, and other controversial leaders get their books published (not that I agreed with everything they wrote, any more than I agree with everything I wrote five years ago).

Tell me, how would *you* sleep tonight if you got a hate letter? I found that I had only a few options: I could stop working, or I could stop listening. Neither option seemed to work especially well. Finally, I realized that the only way to truly deal with angry people is to lovingly engage them in real conversations.

Behind every hate letter I receive, I've discovered, is a hurting person who's upset at God. My writings sometimes simply hit one of his or her hot buttons. In a flash, an angry letter appears in my e-mail in-box. I can choose to ignore it, delete it, or hit Reply and ask a question.

Believing that anger is justified when my vision of God is clouded

FACT OR FEELING?

After graduating into middle school, our oldest daughter, Elizabeth, began exhibiting more than a few signs of moodiness.

Of course, this was to be expected. She was growing, maturing, changing, and becoming more and more her own person. With any change—let alone all the changes a twelve-year-old goes through—our emotions tend to go in a wave pattern. Up one minute. Down the next. Sometimes down more than up.

Still, it's not always easy to respond in a calm, polite, loving manner when your oldest daughter starts accusing you, her father, of "always" doing this and "never" doing that, for as long as she can remember.

Before she went to bed one night, Elizabeth was especially moody. We talked. She poured out her latest complaint against me. I was incredulous. *Does she really believe what she's saying?*

I swallowed hard and then asked a question I've found unlocks a myriad of mixed-up feelings.

"Elizabeth, what you just said—is that true, or is that how you feel?"

It's amazing what an effect this question has during a moment of heated emotions.

"It's how I feel," Elizabeth admitted.

I paused, then asked, "Then what do you think is really true?"

She told me something we both could agree upon instantly: Yes, Dad hadn't responded well in a given situation a few minutes ago.

"I'm sorry I hurt your feelings. Would you please forgive me?" I asked.

I could see a sense of relief come over Elizabeth's face and shoulders. No, my dad doesn't hurt my feelings all the time. The world is a better place, again!

Even as adults, we need to sometimes stop and ask ourselves, *What I'm thinking—is it true, or is it how I'm feeling?*

Without denying our feelings of anger—and sometimes even rage—it's liberating to differentiate those emotions from the larger facts at hand.

Over the years, I've discovered that whenever someone becomes enraged at me, odds are we're only two steps away from becoming good friends.

Why?

First, because that person is emotionally engaged in our relationship. There's passion!

Second, because if true Christianity is about anything, it's about reconciliation. Once a matter is settled, the other person and I are bonded. Sometimes for a while. Sometimes for life.

The same principles apply to a relationship with God. He isn't defensive or threatened when we feel angry at him. After all, we're passionate. And he's equally passionate about being reconciled to us, whether or not we want anything to do with him right now.

God is waiting for us to express our innermost feelings toward him and then ask ourselves, *Is that true, or is that how I feel?*

Sometimes we're not angry with God, it turns out. Instead, we're angry at a caricature of God we've painted like graffiti on the walls of our psyche.

I had a rather intense conversation with a good friend during a time when our church was going through some particularly rough waters. He was railing about "the elders" this and "the elders" that.

I looked at him incredulously. "John, aren't you forgetting something? I'm on the elder board."

John profusely denied he was talking about me, so I pushed the point further.

"Well, who are you talking about then? Paul? Dick? Bob?"

No. No. And no, again.

"John, I'm confused. At the moment, we're the *only* elders at church. If you're not upset with any of us, *who is it?*"

Thunderbolt!

I've had variations of this same conversation through the years. It's amazing to watch the lights go on when someone realizes the anger he or she feels *doesn't equal reality*.

The fact is, we all have internal arguments with projections we've created of someone else. But these projections change our perceptions of the real person and thus complicate our real-life relationships.

Unfortunately, since the let-it-all-hang-out 1960s, our culture has made a religion out of equating *consciousness of feelings* with *reality*. But feelings are only indicators of our perception of reality at any given time.

In every situation, my responses to God and others immediately show my virtue or lack thereof.

MISSING FRUIT

Traditionally, Christian virtues have been called the fruit of the Spirit. Surprisingly, however, after two millennia, Christian art has symbols for only the first three:

- Love—heart
- Joy—oil
- Peace—river

But what about the rest?

- Patience
- Kindness
- Goodness

- Faithfulness
- Gentleness
- Self-control

It seems to me that every one of these virtues is the antithesis of hatred, anger, wrath, and strife. Yet what is the church most known for? For many, the word *Christian* often conjures up images of the Crusades, the Inquisition, and other tragic chapters in world history that haunt us to this day.

Suppose someone from a Muslim country visited a church near you this weekend. How would he or she be greeted? Warmly? Or with suspicion? Since September 11, 2001, I think the latter is more common.

My friend Abraham Sarker found this out the hard way. He gladly shook hands with a church greeter. The greeter's ready smile quickly disappeared, however, when his hand brushed against something hard in Abraham's suit jacket pocket. Immediately, the greeter led Abraham to the side of the foyer and frisked him. The hard object in Abraham's suit turned out to be a cell phone. Still, Abraham felt embarrassed and humiliated. If this had happened a few years ago, Abraham would have walked out of that church and never returned.

Abraham was born into a devout Muslim home in Dhaka, Bangladesh. At age thirteen he joined the Jamaat-e-Islami Party, trained to be a Muslim leader, and successfully began evangelizing people in his own country. At age fifteen, however, Abraham had a terrifying dream about hell, prayed all night, and then heard God tell him, "Go and get a Bible." Abraham's Muslim faith was shaken. Still, at age nineteen, Abraham was sent to the United States on a student visa to help convert Americans to Islam.

Upon arriving in America, Abraham received a Bible in his own language as a gift. Later, an American named Peter befriended

Abraham, heard his claims about Islam, and over time introduced Abraham to the life-changing gospel of Jesus Christ. At first Abraham was skeptical, but he earnestly prayed, "God, lead me in the right direction." Like many Muslims, Abraham wanted to know more about Adam, Noah, Moses, and Jesus, but he was not familiar with their English names (he knew Jesus as "Isa").

Abraham wanted to hear what Peter and others did (and didn't) believe about God, but he reacted negatively if anyone referred to Jesus as "God" or as "the Son of God." Peter realized he had to choose his terms carefully and build on the truth that God is One (as Jesus did repeatedly with the Jewish people).

Eventually, Abraham surprised his friends by committing his life to Jesus Christ. He went on to earn his doctorate at a prestigious Christian university.

Unfortunately, as the story of the cell phone illustrates, this doesn't mean Christian churches always welcome Abraham—or others from Muslim nations—with open arms. Our anger over what a few people did to America has affected our view of an entire people group. It's also affected our relationship with God. In many ways, we've pushed the real God out of the picture.

But there is hope. If we change our minds, reject our angry ways, and choose instead to base our lives on God's love and grace, we can see God clearly again. My wife, Renée, learned this firsthand. Her story, excerpted here, swept across the Internet within hours of 9/11:

> I don't know what I expected when I wandered into
> the Saudi Arabian exhibit at the 1986 World's Fair in
> Vancouver, B.C., but I wasn't there long before I wanted out.
> Brown-uniformed guards watched our every move. Even
> before leaving the oppressive atmosphere of the exhibit,
> I determined Muslims weren't anywhere in my future.

Let other people with different hearts reach out to these people—I didn't want anything to do with them.

Within a year, however, God changed my prejudiced heart. My husband and I wanted to befriend international students, so one Friday evening we visited an international Christian coffeehouse at a nearby university. As soon as we walked in, a friend motioned us over to where he was visiting with two new acquaintances. We sat down opposite this couple, and I found myself greeting a friendly man and his traditionally dressed wife. We chatted and found out that not only were they Muslims, but Hamid and Fatima were from Saudi Arabia. Not only were they from Saudi Arabia, they were from Mecca—Muslims to the core.

Rebuked by visiting relatives for their lack of American friends, Fatima and Hamid were thrilled to meet another couple with children at the coffeehouse. We began to spend time together as friends. That winter we took their family to the mountains to go inner tubing. The next summer we spent a delightful day at the beach. We ate American meals together and enjoyed Fatima's wonderful Arabic cooking.

We began to see Hamid and Fatima not simply as "Muslims" but as unique individuals. Through their friendship we learned to love Muslims the way God did— one at a time.

After we had become good friends, I took the initiative to ask Fatima if she would be willing to study the Koran with me. Not only did I learn the teachings of the Koran, but Fatima took an honest look at her own religious beliefs. "Traditionally, we do not *think* about the Koran," she told me at one point. "We just memorize it." Thinking about the Koran raised issues she had never considered. As we went along, I was able to explain how different stories and teachings coincided or compared with the Bible. And because I was willing to read the Koran, she accepted the Arabic New Testament (*Injil*) I gave her.

Three years after we met, Fatima and her family returned home to the Middle East. We still correspond, and I pray for her often. She made no profession of faith, but I know there is now one woman in Mecca who knows where to go to find Jesus. And when I hear testimonies of Muslims seeking Jesus Christ—who have heard his name via radio or literature and who want to read God's Word—my old fears give way to renewed hope.

God has not called me to go abroad and live among Muslims, but he has opened my heart to care about these people he so dearly loves.

AT THE CROSS

Did you catch the virtues Renée mentions?

Faith. Hope. Love.

According to Paul the apostle, "the greatest of these is love."

This from a man who led the first inquisition against "heretics," the early followers of Jesus Christ.

This from a man who was known for his anger, malice, and rage.

This from a man who applauded the crucifixion of the greatest "heretic" of them all, Jesus Christ.

As I've meditated on the significance of the three crosses where Jesus and two others faced death, I've come to a deeper understanding of the three ways humanity faces the inevitable.

Like the first thief. We can act as if we can't see God—allowing our feelings of anger and spite to cloud our vision of reality.

Like the second thief. We can rise above our feelings and see the reality that the God of the universe is with us and we can experience hope in our darkest hour.

Except for those brief minutes between their deaths, Jesus offered his presence to the dying thief. Only after taking him to God the Father's presence did Jesus return to earth to spend forty more days with his followers.

I find it more than a matter of fact that Jesus disappeared for the second thief for a short period and then for almost six weeks following the thief's conversion. Of course, whether those six weeks were measurable in light of the eternalness of heaven is debatable. Perhaps that absence felt like only a matter of minutes. Still . . .

Jesus made incredible promises to the second thief, only to disappear. Somehow, it almost strikes me as abandonment. Yet was it? What if the Lord isn't quite as worried about disappearing as we are?

It sounds almost wrong to say such a thing. Or perhaps I'm stretching one incident beyond the scope of Jesus' later promise to be with his followers "always, even to the end of the age."

Or is it possible that the promise is bigger than minutes, hours, days, even weeks and months? During World War II, was it bigger than years? During and after the Black Plague, was it bigger than decades? After the fall of the Roman Empire, was it bigger than centuries?

There's a third lesson about facing the inevitable that we can learn from the Cross:

Like Jesus. In Jesus' own experience on the cross, we discover something shocking. God the Father removed his intentional, tangible presence (his face) from the Lord Jesus. What gave God the Father the right to do that? For what purpose? If we discover the shocking reason, I believe you and I will have the possibility of understanding God the Father's divine right—and purpose—in disappearing for a time in our lives as well.

The shocking reason is this: Only when God disappears can we fully enter into his terrible sufferings.

The Lord's sufferings include much more than the cross. They also include the tens of billions of years collectively that humanity has turned its back on the maker of heaven and earth.

To say "tens of billions of years" is verifiable by analyzing and extrapolating the best empirical data measuring unbelief and disbelief among the population in each nation over the past century alone.

To say "tens of billions" sounds shocking, but it's true.

If we (humanity) have shut out God from our hearts and minds that much, is it too much for us to enter into his terrible sufferings for an infinitely small period of time?

I'm asking a real question, knowing that for some the time is measured by months or years, not days or weeks.

At one point my friend Dean angrily asked me why God did not protect a close friend, Susie, from being murdered. Susie had repeatedly told Dean and others how God delivered her from her husband's drug-induced murderous threats. Sometimes when he was threatening and intimidating her, he would suddenly just stop, look confused, and move away. It was almost as if God clouded his mind so that he could not proceed. And yet one time the power of evil prevailed.

My friends Don and Lisa walked not one but two daughters through teenage pregnancy. Both Don and Lisa felt deeply angry: "God, this is not part of our plan—why is it yours? Why did you let this happen?"

On top of everything else, my friends felt judged by some of their fellow church members, who responded as if Don and Lisa had sinned and God had walked away from their family. Frequent misguided and often judgmental statements hit the family from all sides.

"There were times we wanted to turn and run," Don tells me. But they remained steadfast in their belief that God loves them, realizing that reality is so much more than the feelings of hurt and anger they were dealing with in that situation.

To me, these two stories present a stark contrast. I see lives marked by grace and other lives marked by a denial of grace.

When we harbor unrelenting anger, we're really denying God. Grace, however, is an encounter with God as he truly is. I believe he's a God well acquainted with sorrow. Why? So we can experience his grace.

Experiencing the power of love with grace

FAITH BUILDER

THE POWER OF LOVE

The night before his crucifixion, Jesus wasted no time in communicating what was foremost on his heart and mind.

To show them the full extent of his love, Jesus washed the disciples' feet, ate the Jewish Passover meal with them, and—using the bread and cup—shared the first Christian Communion with them. After dismissing Judas the betrayer, Jesus told his disciples one more time that he must die for their sins.

Then Jesus said something startling, revolutionary, and in many ways world changing.

First, Jesus said, "So now I am giving you a new commandment" (John 13:34).

Peter, James, John, and the other disciples must have sat up

61

when Jesus made this proclamation. They'd followed Jesus Christ closely for three and a half years. They'd seen virtually every miracle, heard almost every word of Jesus. Now, with the Cross only hours away, the tension surely rose in that room. I wonder if everyone was holding his breath. You can almost feel the sense of anticipation. What was Jesus going to say next?

What Jesus said next was this: "Love each other."

You can almost imagine Jesus pausing to let those words sink in. Of course, the more they sunk in, the more the disciples must have wrinkled their foreheads. *Love each other?* That's it?

I can almost hear Thomas muttering under his breath, "Well, Jesus, so it's true after all. Everything I needed to know I learned in kindergarten. What in the world are you talking about? Moses gave us the commandment to 'love your neighbor as yourself' almost 1,500 years ago. You can't get much *older* than that."

That would have been a good point—*if* Jesus meant only for us to love each other as we love ourselves. But Jesus wasn't finished yet.

He went on to say, "Just as I have loved you, you should love each other."

In eleven crisp, clear words, Jesus radically changed what it means to love another human being. No longer is it enough to love someone as much as I love myself.

Of course, that's hard enough horizontally. But Jesus has flipped everything vertically.

It's no longer enough for me to love others horizontally, that is, as much as I love myself. Instead, I need to love them vertically, as much as Jesus loves us.

Furthermore, Jesus said, "Your love for one another will prove to the world that you are my disciples" (John 13:35).

Everything good that Christianity has done in the past two thousand years has been the fruit of our love for one another. Conversely, everything evil that people have done in the name of

Jesus Christ—blaspheming his holy name—has been the fruit of rejecting what Jesus Christ said, especially in these two verses.

I don't care how much such people talk about love. "Love" divorced from God's grace isn't love at all. Conversely, love with grace makes all the difference in the world.

On your favorite search engine, type in "John 13:34-35" and "William Wilberforce" or "Mother Teresa" or even "Billy Graham." You'll find hundreds of links. Each of these people had a monumental, positive impact on the world. What was their secret? May I suggest it isn't a secret at all? They simply knew how to love others as Jesus did: on the basis of Jesus' righteousness, filled with Jesus' grace, year after year, decade after decade—until the whole world *knew* they were Jesus' disciples.

When Jesus used the phrase, "your love . . . will prove," he wasn't talking about some kind of intellectual accomplishment. Instead, the upper room discourse, as John 13–17 is often called, shows how the fruit of our love can become a phenomenal display of the Lord's glory in the world. And what is the fruit of loving as Jesus loved? We find the answer right in the Scripture text.

The fruit of loving is obeying Jesus, just as Jesus obeyed his Father to the point of being willing to lay down his life for us. This is the fruit of *sacrifice*.

The fruit of loving as Jesus loved us is experiencing unity with God and with each other. This is the fruit of *intimacy*, spiritually and relationally.

The fruit of intimacy and the fruit of sacrifice are inseparable. Together, they become an incredible display of the Lord's glory in the world.

Of course, this all sounds good. But do we have any evidence that the disciples actually took Jesus' new commandment to heart? Let's take a look.

First, we find similar injunctions in the writings of Peter, James,

John, and Paul. In fact, John and Paul talked constantly about it, as we'll see in a minute.

Even more important, each of the apostles, to his dying day, was renowned for an intimate walk with God, a passion for unity within the church, and sacrificial love. To a man, each was willing to die a martyr's death, following the example of his Lord and Savior. They took the gospel of Jesus Christ west from Antioch to Spain and east from Jerusalem to India and later to China.

What compelled these men to give the rest of their lives, year after year, decade after decade, to the Lord's service?

Beyond the example of the apostles, our attention is drawn back to the amazing, intimate, sacrificial love that God the Father and Jesus demonstrated to us and to the rest of the world.

The apostle John wrote about this in verse after verse in the letter we now call 1 John. John couldn't get over the amazing love of God the Father and Jesus his Son. Take a minute to drink in these words:

> Dear friends, let us continue to love one another, for love comes from God. Anyone who loves is a child of God and knows God. But anyone who does not love does not know God, for God is love.   *1 John 4:7-8*

But John kept writing:

> God showed how much he loved us by sending his one and only Son into the world so that we might have eternal life through him. This is real love—not that we loved God, but that he loved us and sent his Son as a sacrifice to take away our sins.   *1 John 4:9-10*

Still, John didn't stop:

> Dear friends, since God loved us that much, we surely ought to love each other. No one has ever seen God.

> But if we love each other, God lives in us, and his love is
> brought to full expression in us.   *1 John 4:11-12*

John continued to write about this amazing love for four more paragraphs in that chapter alone and in dozens of other passages throughout his writings.

Likewise, the apostle Paul couldn't seem to keep from writing about the amazing, intimate, sacrificial love of God the Father and Jesus his Son. Paul constantly marveled that God demonstrated the full extent of his love by giving his Son, who in turn gave his life for us. Paul shined the light of Jesus' love through the prism of his classic words in 1 Corinthians 13, which are so often read at weddings.

It was to this high standard of love—Jesus' own love—that the aged apostle Paul appealed when he wrote to his dear friend Philemon. In that short letter, which is a majestic example of persuasive writing, Paul urged Philemon to spare the life of his runaway slave, Onesimus, and instead embrace him as a new brother in Jesus Christ.

So, did Jesus' new commandment make any difference in the lives of the apostles and the early church? To say the least, we can give a loud, resounding yes! But what about the other key question we need to ask ourselves? Can Jesus' new commandment make any real difference in our lives?

Again, I think the answer is yes.

Think of the energy exerted by the crowd at a sold-out concert or an exciting sporting event. Think of the even greater amount of energy exerted by someone who serves God and others faithfully year after year, decade after decade. When you think how much God loves us, how much energy are you willing to expend loving other people? How intimate are you willing to be? How much are you willing to sacrifice?

More specifically, whom are you choosing to love? Does anyone come to mind? Who is he? Who is she? Say that person's name in your mind. Say, *Yes, Lord, I'm choosing to love* _____. It may mean getting to know that person better. It may mean sacrificing something. Whom are you choosing to love?

Perhaps you're thinking of someone whose health has been poor or a friend who lives overseas. Or perhaps you're thinking about someone who serves others quietly behind the scenes, without applause or fanfare. Maybe it's a family member or someone you have a hard time getting along with.

In a world that's often raging mad, God's love infused with grace is the one thing that really matters here and for eternity.

EVERYONE LOVES DREAMS of "getting away from it all."

Dreams turn to nightmares, however, if we get lost and can't find our way back.

The first time I lost someone I was eight. My brother, four friends, and I were playing in the woods. Our adventure soon turned into a full-scale World War II battle scene. What we lacked in equipment we more than made up for with vivid imaginations and our best sound effects.

It was all great fun until one of my friends started shouting for his little brother, Danny Paul. We searched everywhere. Panicked, we finally ran to Danny Paul's house and breathlessly told his mother what had happened. She burst out crying. A minute later she was on the phone to the sheriff.

An hour later the sheriff and his deputies called in a search-and-rescue squad from a nearby military base. Soon a full-scale search was on, complete with an ominous helicopter flying overhead.

My brother remembered we had passed an abandoned well in the woods. Within thirty minutes, they had found it and sent someone down the shaft. Nothing.

Another hour passed. Still no sign of Danny Paul.

Overcome with despair, his mother walked sobbing into his bedroom, grieving the loss of her little boy. There he lay asleep on top of his bed.

Afterward, I often marveled at how serious grown-ups can get when someone is missing but then forget to look in the most obvious of places.

If I neglect time with God long enough, I may not know how to readily connect with him again.

Have you lost your connection with God at any point in the past?

Have you seen others lose their faith, disappearing into agnosticism or unbelief? If so, did they ever come back?

FAITH WRECKER Neglecting my time with God and failing to see him in my life

FAITH SLIPPING AWAY

Shortly before his crucifixion, Jesus asked, "When the Son of Man returns, how many will he find on the earth who have faith?"

For some reason, we've bought into the idea that the correct answer is none, but that's the opposite of what the New Testament teaches.

Read the Gospels of Matthew, Mark, Luke, and John. Jesus goes on at length to teach us that the end will not come until his Good News is preached throughout the world. Yes, false religions and persecutions will abound. Many Christians will let their faith grow cold. But the fact is, Jesus specifically and clearly told his followers to "go and make disciples of all the nations."

Until a generation ago, we didn't know what our own planet looked like from above. Now, whenever I like, I can instantly look at detailed aerial and satellite photos of my neighborhood. If I zoom in far enough, I can even see two white cars in my driveway, my huge blue recycling container and smaller black garbage can on wheels at the curb, and the small pond in my backyard. I half expect to see my two youngest kids running around. It's a bit eerie, to say the least.

I wonder how God sees my neighborhood. After all, if he made the universe(s), he's *huge*. I'm not thinking about quantity or size. Instead, I'm thinking about quality or greatness. Of course, what if I could see God looking at me? Would I shake my fist or smile and wave?

When I visit the great cities of Europe or Latin America, I can't resist walking around and into the old cathedrals. The buildings themselves are designed to provoke a religious experience, a sense of awe at the greatness of God above.

I used to wonder how we could have the audacity to think that such a huge God penetrated all the galaxies to be near us. I then realized the error of such thinking, as if value is determined by size, when in fact the entire universe is nothing compared to God. It's amazing that he's interested in *anything*. Yet an ancient writer assures us that God is indeed mindful of us. We live on a visited planet.

Interestingly, Jesus associated with the high and mighty only during infancy (the Magi) and shortly before his death (Pilate and Herod)—both times in circumstances that appeared out of his control.

Mostly, Jesus associated with people like you and me. God came near. God still comes near. To many in the Islamic world, he comes in dreams. To many in the postmodern West, he comes in any of a hundred everyday disguises.

If we have prefabricated ideas about how Jesus has to show up to be real, we're setting ourselves up for disappointment.

God does more than show up at weddings and funerals, nature shows and the Weather Channel. The bass guitarist for a local band was surprised to see Jesus show up at a recent Rickie Lee Jones concert. Another friend found God waiting tables in college. Still others came to faith through the birth of their first child.

When was the last time you felt God's presence, his reality? What sparked that experience? Were you surprised?

If it's been a long time, you may have experienced a lot of pain. If so, it's pretty hard to believe anything I might say about God's promises, isn't it?

FAMILY PROMISES

When we adopted our youngest daughter, Anna, we promised she would be part of our family forever. The first few weeks and months she was with us, we had to repeat that promise frequently. Why? Because of the terrible wounds in her heart, Anna couldn't believe us. In some ways beyond her control or understanding, she still may not believe us.

Family relationships are formed in one of two ways. Either someone is born into a family or someone makes a promise. It might be a wedding vow or an adoption decree, but a solemn promise is made to another person. The promise is often blessed by God, recognized by the governing authorities, and celebrated by the extended family, church, and broader community of friends and neighbors.

Interestingly, Scripture contains relatively few promises by individuals to God, and frankly half of those are lame or foolish. Instead, what we mostly find in the Bible are hundreds of promises that God has made to people. Specifically, we find four types of promises God makes by his grace, and each is relational in nature.

Ultimately, these promises all have to do with bringing people into God's family.

First, there are the promises God made over thousands of years about the Messiah, Jesus Christ, the one the Bible calls our Lord and Savior. Second, there are the promises God made to the Israelites, in both the Hebrew and Christian Scriptures.

Third, there are the promises God made about and to the Gentiles, inviting them to be his people. Fourth, there are the promises God made in the New Testament to the church, to all the followers of Jesus Christ throughout the ages—since Jesus Christ's resurrection and ascension and the Holy Spirit's filling of all believers on the Day of Pentecost.

Interestingly, actually amazingly, the Bible makes it a point to describe believers in each group as adopted "children of the promise."

Like Anna, however, most of us don't believe our heavenly Father's promises.

You would think that some of the dramatic stories of the Bible or the incredible prophecies about the future would be the most difficult for people to believe.

Instead, in my experience, it seems that people have the greatest problem believing the promises of God. Oh, they sound nice, and sometimes they even cheer us up. But we wonder, *Do they really work?* Unconsciously, at least, we question whether or not God keeps his promises.

Of course, we absolutely have to wrestle with this essential, core question of the Christian faith. But if we only question flippantly or halfheartedly, or with the cynical attitude that God's Word doesn't have any answers, we may risk inflicting damage to our souls.

In the Bible, after all, we can read true accounts of real men and women who genuinely struggled to prove whether or not God keeps his promises. Such proof doesn't come easily. It's not an intellectual decision. It's proved in the life choices we make and the record of what God accomplishes in and through our lives.

In the Old Testament, Joshua could declare near the end of his life that "not a single one of all the good promises the LORD had given to the family of Israel was left unfulfilled." A short time later, Joshua reminded all the leaders of Israel: "Deep in your hearts you know that every promise of the LORD your God has come true. Not a single one has failed!" That's quite a remarkable declaration from a man who followed God for about a century.

During the middle of his life, King Solomon echoed the words of Joshua, telling the whole nation of Israel: "Praise the LORD who has given rest to his people Israel, just as he promised. Not one word has failed of all the wonderful promises he gave through his servant Moses."

Of course, if we don't guard our hearts, like Solomon we, too, can lose our faith during the second half of our lives, as we've already seen.

Yet the record stands all through the ages: None of God's promises have ever failed. Think about it. How is that possible? It's possible because the fulfillment of those promises is dependent on God, not on us. God is faithful, at the very core of his being, so he has never once failed to keep his word.

Instead, God has gone on record many times throughout the Bible to give us—his much-loved adopted children—what the apostle Peter calls "great and precious promises."

Of course, some of God's promises through the ages have been made to specific individuals, to particular groups, or to an ancient nation. So we must be very careful not to haphazardly claim promises God intended for someone else. We also can't miss the fact that some of God's promises in the past were conditional, especially some of his promises to the ancient Israelite nation.

Thankfully, many of God's Old Testament promises—about his gracious character and love and care for his people—are repeated in the New Testament and are ours to claim today. For instance, God promised Joshua, "I will not fail you or abandon you." In the New Testament, God transfers that promise to us as the newest members of his family.

Over the centuries, millions of followers of Jesus Christ have made a habit of underlining God's promises in the Bible. It's a habit you may want to practice as well. Just be careful not to haphazardly take Scripture verses out of context. If a promise isn't clearly based on a proper understanding of God's Word, and if it doesn't apply to millions of other followers of Jesus Christ, then it isn't a promise of God you and I can claim.

When we do identify genuine promises that apply to millions of followers of Christ, we also need to understand how those promises fit into God's grand scheme of things.

Some of God's promises, of course, will be fulfilled only in the future. But many of God's promises are true the moment we accept his invitation to become his children. In fact, they're true whether or not we—like children adopted as infants or toddlers— even know about the promises. They're also true no matter how long ago God made them.

Many other promises of God will be fulfilled during the course of our lives, whether or not we see the fulfillment. At the end of his life, for instance, Peter reminded us that God "does not want anyone to be destroyed, but wants everyone to repent." That verse doesn't promise that everyone will go to heaven against his or her will. But it does promise us that God doesn't want anyone to go to hell. Instead, he wants people to change their minds about their sin and need for the Savior. The reality is, God can work in someone's heart even at the last hour, whether we know it or not.

So often, however, we lose faith when a friend or loved one

doesn't follow Jesus Christ—year after year, decade after decade. Nothing I do can force God to fulfill one of his promises. Nothing. Instead, I'm entirely dependent on him. Thankfully, our God is trustworthy and faithful. As the apostle Paul was able to say: What we know and believe rests on the "confidence that they have eternal life, which God—who does not lie—promised them before the world began."

The reality is, we can count on God's promises to meet our every need. But we must ask for his provision, trust him, and wait. I can do the first part. Sometimes I can do the second part. But that third part—waiting—isn't always easy. In fact, it can grind up my faith if I'm not careful. Yet persistence, endurance, and waiting are spiritual facts of life.

In Matthew 7:7—one of my life verses—Jesus says, "Keep on asking, and you will receive what you ask for. Keep on seeking, and you will find. Keep on knocking, and the door will be opened to you."

In other verses, we are told that any promises we can claim in Jesus' name—that is, any promises God has made to us as his adopted children—are guaranteed and will be fulfilled for us by God for his glory. We just have to wait.

FAITH BUILDER — Reclaiming God's promises even if I have to wait

WAITING FOR CHRISTMAS

Have you ever thought about the fact that good things, including Christmas, are mostly about waiting?

The story of Christmas actually begins in the Garden of Eden. When Adam and Eve ate fruit from the tree of the knowledge of good and evil, God didn't panic. Heaven didn't go on red alert. God had seen this coming long before Creation. God searched for Adam and Eve, found them, and sacrificed animals to clothe them. Then he went on record foretelling a coming Messiah who would crush Satan's head and bring deliverance to God's people. And then, maybe even with tears running down his cheeks, God dismissed Adam and Eve from the Garden.

I can almost see God standing by the forbidden tree, knowing that one day he himself would return to earth disguised as a human baby. Knowing that he would grow up and be nailed to a tree, bearing all the evil and sin and wickedness of this world in his own body. And by doing so, in the moment of Satan's greatest triumph, he would turn around and crush Satan and rise from the dead to offer new life, eternal life, to all who believe.

God stooped to join the human family that we might be lifted up to join his. God was born as the seed of woman that we might be adopted as his own sons and daughters. God became sin that we might take on his righteousness. By his wounds we were healed.

Yet this promise of the coming Messiah was made thousands of years before Jesus Christ's birth.

If we miss this, we miss the whole point of Christmas—Christmas is about an incredible promise God made to us that took thousands of years to be fulfilled.

It's about promise and about waiting a very, very long time.

Don't get me wrong. At the right time, Jesus Christ was born. God added more than sixty prophecies to his original one, telling his people precisely when, where, and why Jesus Christ would be born.

The miracle isn't that a handful of shepherds and wise men came to worship the newborn King of kings, but that the whole world didn't flock to Bethlehem to greet his entrance into the world.

Not one member of the Jewish ruling council, not one rabbi, not one priest took the time to walk an hour and a half from

Jerusalem to Bethlehem to see the Word become flesh, to see God dwelling again with humanity.

At the end of the Old Testament, God makes this sobering declaration: "I will search with lanterns in Jerusalem's darkest corners to punish those who sit complacent in their sins. They think the LORD will do nothing to them, either good or bad." Yet in the end, not even the high priest himself welcomed baby Jesus into the world.

The high priest probably didn't believe God was going to do anything here on earth, either good or bad, to change the status quo. After all, God hadn't done anything, as far as he could tell, for centuries. The heavens were silent. The prophets spoke no more. No one had seen a miracle since the days of the Maccabees. For all practical purposes, God had disappeared.

Oh, many Jewish people back then were devout. Don't get me wrong. But many were Jewish in name only.

The apostle John said, "He came to his own people, and even they rejected him. But to all who believed him and accepted him, he gave the right to become children of God."

Who were some of those who received Jesus and believed on his name?

In Luke chapter 2, we have the famous Christmas story about Joseph and Mary traveling from Nazareth to Bethlehem, the city of David, when Caesar Augustus issued a decree that a census should be taken of the entire Roman Empire.

If you keep reading that chapter, you find that forty days after Jesus' birth, Joseph and Mary went to Jerusalem to consecrate Jesus. There they met Simeon, who had been promised by God that he would see the Messiah in his own lifetime.

The Holy Spirit was upon Simeon. He was filled with God. Still, he longed to see the Christ child. The day he took Jesus in his arms, I can imagine him laughing, looking, wondering: *God, is that you?*

Against all odds, at the end of Simeon's life, God had kept his promise.

WAITING

Interestingly, it appears that Jesus never told his disciples to "wait" until after his resurrection. He did, however, tell them to wait for the Holy Spirit, who would come on the day of Pentecost.

The apostle Paul didn't talk much about waiting either. But when he did, he always talked about waiting in hope of Jesus Christ's return. How? Each time, Paul made a point of saying that the Holy Spirit is the one who enables us to wait. In Ephesians 1:13-14, he spoke of the promised Holy Spirit, referring to the promise that one day we will be joined with God in heaven.

Waiting doesn't come naturally. We hate to wait. To wait for Jesus Christ's return, we need the Holy Spirit's supernatural power. If we quench the Holy Spirit, if we grieve him, if we tune him out of our lives, or if we think the Lord will never come back, we won't have the power we need to continue waiting.

And when we stop waiting, we run the risk of calling God a liar. We run the risk of of thinking, *God, I don't care how incredible it was that Jesus came the first time. It's been two thousand years. I'm giving up. I'm doing my own thing.*

Yet anything worth having is worth waiting for. Anybody can walk down the aisle, but it takes a lifetime to produce a good marriage. Likewise, we can't be holy in a hurry. There are no shortcuts to spiritual maturity. Most of faith is patience, waiting.

But it's so hard to wait, isn't it?

THEO'S BOOTS

Outside, revelers paraded down the narrow streets of a small European town in celebration of Fasching, the Tuesday before Ash

Wednesday and the start of Lent, known in other parts of the world as Mardi Gras.

Inside his home, Theo labored for each breath. He was prepared to pass from this life into the next, but he needed to do one more thing.

Leaning over to his wife, he whispered, "Christa, show Scott that picture of Anton."

My close friend Scott studied the black-and-white photo before handing it back. "I'm afraid I don't know this man," he said.

"I didn't think you would," Theo said. "I just wanted you to see his face so if you ever saw him, you could speak with him."

The man was Anton Fishbach, a school friend of Theo's who directed a traditional religious institution in Vienna. Theo had spoken to him about his faith in Jesus Christ and the vibrant church he and Christa were attending, but Anton had never come to know Jesus as Theo had. Assured that Scott would continue talking to Anton about God's gift of eternal life, Theo died with a smile on his lips and joy in his heart.

As Christa cleaned out Theo's belongings, she determined that Scott should receive his leather boots. "I would rather you have them than give them to someone I don't know," she said. Scott was glad to receive this visual reminder of his friend.

Theo's funeral was held on a cold, snowy Friday afternoon. At the cemetery, after a few words of committal, everyone followed the tradition of filing by the grave site, taking a shovelful of dirt, and tossing it onto the casket that had been lowered into the burial pit.

Hundreds of people merged into two lines, and Scott became separated from his wife. He glanced at the man next to him. It was Anton—the man from Theo's photo!

Theo had charged him with speaking to Anton if he ever had the opportunity, but to start a conversation at this somber moment would break an Austrian tradition. Scott said nothing as they inched their way toward the grave.

When they reached the grave site, Scott allowed Anton to go first. He made the sign of the cross and uttered a few words that Scott couldn't hear. Then Scott, wearing Theo's boots, stepped up to the side of the grave, tossed a spadeful of dirt on the casket, and caught up with Anton.

"Are you Herr Fishbach?" he asked.

"Yes," he said, obviously surprised. "Do I know you?"

"No, but I know you. Just before he died, Theo told me he felt very burdened for you and often prayed for you. He also showed me your picture and asked me to talk with you should I ever see you."

"This is amazing," Anton said. "Absolutely amazing."

"Yes, it is amazing," agreed Scott, "especially when you see how many friends Theo had."

"Tell me, why was Theo so concerned about me?"

"You know about his faith, don't you?"

Anton nodded.

"You see, Theo had absolute certainty that he would go directly to be with the Lord when he died. In fact, at the end he had a deep longing to see Jesus Christ."

"Yes, Theo was a man of deep faith," Anton said.

"The thing that concerned him, however, was that he wasn't sure if he would see you in heaven."

Anton's mouth fell open. He began fishing around in his pockets until he pulled out a card. "Here is my phone number in Vienna. I will be out of town next week, but please call me. I must talk to you about these things."

About ten days later, they met again in Anton's office.

"Anton, I think you would agree that the Lord has orchestrated many events in the last weeks to bring me here today," Scott said.

"I would ask that the normal reserve we would have for each other in a meeting like this would evaporate this afternoon. May I have your permission to speak directly?"

"By all means," said Anton.

Scott explained to Anton that the only way to heaven was to trust Jesus Christ as his Lord and Savior—that no amount of effort or good deeds could get him there. Anton began asking questions, so many that he called his secretary and asked her to cancel his next appointment.

Scott left Anton's office that day unsure what Anton would choose to believe. A glance down at his boots—Theo's boots—reminded him, however, that God was in control. Theo's prayers would be answered in *God's* time.

MR. YANAGISAWA'S STORY

Sixty-three-year-old Akira Yanagisawa wondered why he had worked so hard all of his life. What did he really have to show for forty-plus years of labor?

As a young man he worked for Unisys and serviced Toyota Motor Corporation's 20-million-dollar supercomputer. After doing that for thirty years, he took early retirement and started his own computer company.

On his way to work one day, he noticed a new building going up. Each day he followed its progress, wondering what it might be. When atop the steel frame he noticed a white cross, he no longer had to guess what it would be. He decided he would attend the church.

The first week he sat near the back. When the worship service was over, he was quick to slip out. After a few weeks, an acquaintance of mine in Japan, Mennonite pastor Laurence Hiebert, managed to intercept him before his speedy departure. He was surprised to find that Mr. Yanagisawa was eager to set up an appointment to talk.

Sitting in Laurence's office later that week, Mr. Yanagisawa shared that his ninety-three-year-old mother had suffered a severe stroke and was on her deathbed. He wondered if Laurence would assist with funeral preparations. His ninety-seven-year-old father was also recovering from a recent fall. Each Sunday he hurried home to prepare lunch for his father and then visited his mother.

Later that day, Laurence went to visit Mr. Yanagisawa's mother. She was frail and clearly near death. Sustained by oxygen, she groaned with each breath. He sat by her hospital bed, read Psalm 23, and prayed for her. He noticed that Mr. Yanagisawa's hands were white knuckled as he prayed along in earnest.

As they left the room, Mr. Yanagisawa said solemnly, "It seems we'd better start planning for a funeral." Laurence assured him that the church was willing to help. But because he was not a Christian, Mr. Yanagisawa felt it would be too much to ask to have the funeral at the church. Instead he planned to hold it at a friend's funeral home and asked Laurence to assist him in the preparations. Over the next week they planned the program. Mr. Yanagisawa, being adept at computers, prepared an eight-page funeral program with color pictures and his mother's life history. The only thing missing was the date of her death.

Over the next several months Mr. Yanagisawa regularly attended church and finally indicated that he wanted to yield his life to Jesus. Laurence studied the Bible with him and prepared him for baptism. On the day of his baptism Mr. Yanagisawa placed his laptop computer on the pulpit and told his Christian testimony via a PowerPoint presentation.

He explained that his parents had come to Jesus Christ and had been baptized seventy years earlier. His father had served at a church and even lived in the church building.

Tragically, as a result of the reconstruction after World War II, their church building was destroyed and their congregation disbanded. Their family moved to Toyota City, but because there were no churches there yet, they were no longer regular in church attendance. They did attend an occasional Bible study or church in a neighboring town, however, and sometimes Mr. Yanagisawa even attended with them.

Yet not even a brush with death was enough to cause him to commit his life to Jesus Christ. He told the congregation about his university days when he was a member of a mountain-climbing club. One day nine members went climbing but only two returned. He showed a picture of himself standing beside the frozen body of one of the climbers caught in the avalanche. "The question on my heart was, *Why did I survive?*" he said.

Later in life, he was in a terrible car accident and should have died, but once again Mr. Yanagisawa's life was spared. Again he wondered why. Fifteen years after the car accident, he collapsed at work, and tests revealed that he still had internal injuries from the car accident. Again God had spared his life.

That's when he began to wonder why he had worked so hard and what he had to show for it that would really last. When he saw the church building going up, he decided to pursue Jesus, even though his parents had lost sight of God some years ago.

During the months leading up to Mr. Yanagisawa's baptism, God's gracious hand had been on his mother. She regained consciousness and gradually began to grow stronger. Then the day came when Laurence knew she could hear him pray. Later she started responding affirmatively to his questions. "Do you believe Jesus? Do you love Jesus?" Each time Laurence came to visit her, tears came to her eyes and she would thank him for coming. One day she said, "I'm looking forward to seeing Jesus." So on the day her son was baptized, she also became a member of the church.

As I write this chapter, Mr. Yanagisawa's mother sits in a wheelchair in a senior-care facility and is able to feed herself again. Not only has God given healing to her body, he has revived her faith that had grown weak and cold. Just when it seemed her life here on earth was over and just as her son began to reflect deeply on his life, God reappeared on the scene.

Mr. Yanagisawa's father is now almost one hundred years old, and he is weaker than his wife. But his weathered hands once again page through his well-worn Bible and hymnbook. His heart is once again responsive to the God he served as a young man. He understands that God never left him. Both he and his wife have returned to the God they loved as a young couple.

What's your story? Have you ever lost your way spiritually? If so, have you come back to God yet? If not, do you want to come back to God? Perhaps not yet. That's fine. For now, God's willing to wait.

EVERYONE LOVES to get lost in music.

But because musical tastes vary widely, one person's music is sometimes another person's noise. My own preferences cover a wide and eclectic spectrum. On more than one occasion, my wife has either winced or smiled when I've shared a new song or CD with our kids. In the end, however, it's been fun to watch them explore different genres and discover their own musical tastes.

When it comes to faith and spirituality, even though my interests are wide, my preferences are pretty narrow. In the end, I rejected atheism (and all of its saints, accepted truths, and dictates) and embraced what some call a new kind of Christianity. That doesn't make me closed-minded, nor does it mean that I hate those who disagree with me. It simply means I have no desire to be a spiritual surfer or religious schizophrenic.

Many people argue that followers of Jesus Christ shouldn't be so "dogmatic" in our belief that he is the only way to God. In fact, even though one of Jesus' most famous sayings, "You will know the truth, and the truth will set you free," is inscribed in stone at several Ivy League universities, it seems that today's culture has turned its meaning around. Many would rather the verse said, "If you think you know the truth, keep it to yourself."

Over the years, not only have I studied Christianity in depth, but I've also explored all the other major religions of the world. I've interviewed people who represent a wide range of beliefs, and I've made many friends along the way. None of that makes me an expert, of course. It doesn't even guarantee I've grown in my faith.

Depending on several factors, the intense exploration of faith issues can draw us closer to God or make us more acutely aware that we can't find him.

In any case, I often tell new acquaintances who want to talk about faith and spirituality that I'd prefer to be a facilitator—not an "answer man"—when it comes to discussing their many questions. In the end, after all, it doesn't matter what I think or believe. So I ask them not to take anything I say as gospel truth.

Instead, I encourage everyone I meet to ask God to show them the truth about their questions and the assumptions behind them. Toward that end, I sometimes suggest the following prayer:

> *Dear God, maker of heaven and earth, please help me to come to the place of knowing you as you are. Help me to come to the place of peace, a peace that passes all understanding, a peace that only you can give. Speak to me in a new way as I read the Bible, your Holy Scriptures. Help me to trust in you on a whole new level, both on my best days and my worst.*

When I first met Fernando, he was a syncretistic believer. That is, he read from a wide assortment of scriptures representing all the world's great religions. I've rarely met such an earnest seeker of truth.

At one point, Fernando began praying the prayer I quoted above. He even had the audacity to note what day he started praying and what day he wanted God to answer him. He was thrilled when God beat that deadline by twenty-three days. Still, Fernando would be the first person to admit he doesn't have a corner on the truth.

Another acquaintance, Karina, has long wrestled with matters of faith. It's difficult for her to find the answers she's looking for. That's okay. I find her questions sincere, honest, and important to ponder. Questions about apparent errors in the Bible. Questions about the age of the universe.

A few months ago I shared a vegetarian pizza and some good conversation with Abhi, a California Polytechnic computer engineering major who grew up in a Hindu family. He asked about my decision to become a lifelong follower of Jesus Christ when I was thirteen. After hearing my story, he scoffed, "You hardly knew anything." I had to agree.

To Abhi, Christianity didn't make sense. Besides, it has too many rules, he thought. It definitely was not music to his ears. I appreciated Abhi's honest admission that he still needed to read the Bible, which I encouraged him to do with one of his Christian friends. Most important, I'm glad Abhi wants to set a date for getting together again the next time I'm in San Luis Obispo, California, visiting my oldest son, Jon.

Maybe like Abhi, you haven't read the Bible yet. Or maybe like Jon, you've read it many times. Friends have sometimes asked me, "How did you convince Jon to read the Bible cover to cover so many times?" The point is, I didn't convince him. He had to make that decision himself. Otherwise, in the end, he likely would have rejected that decision and been tempted to jettison my faith.

What was your experience growing up? Did you have an atheistic father like mine? Or perhaps a father who let you choose your own faith and practices? Or a father who tried to force you to study and accept and follow the dictates of his religion? The latter can be dangerous.

GOD HAS NO GRANDCHILDREN

Only minutes after Jon was born, Renée and I prayed for him, dedicating him to God. Thereafter, we prayed frequently that Jon would grow up to be a man who loved God with all his heart, soul, strength, and mind, and love others as himself.

The answer to that prayer isn't always a given.

A father can have a tremendous positive or negative influence on his child's faith. That influence includes how he approaches the study of faith issues, but it goes far deeper than that. In the end, does he actively encourage or discourage heart devotion to God?

Dr. Paul C. Vitz, professor of psychology at New York University and former atheist, is the author of *Faith of the Fatherless*. In this thought-provoking book, Vitz diagnoses the root causes of atheism and agnosticism. After studying the biographies of many of the leading atheists of the past three centuries, Vitz concludes that virtually all had an absent, distant, harassed, or abusive father very early in their childhood—often before eighteen months of age.[1]

In other words, classic atheism isn't an intellectual decision that God the Father doesn't exist. Instead, it's a reaction against one's earthly father and whatever the son or daughter thought the father stood for.

Three years before Dr. Vitz's findings were published, Luis Palau and I noted the same phenomenon in our book, *God Is Relevant*. We observed, "Huxley, Nietzsche, and Freud, among others, felt a great deal of animosity or hatred toward their fathers, almost all of whom were religious men exhibiting some fault their sons found intolerable."[2]

We added, "Psychological research by William Glasser and

others suggests that severe parent-child alienation often produces negative long-term effects, which was certainly the case for each of these men."[3]

The bottom line? A bad father-child relationship can produce long-lasting spiritual damage in the life of the child. That damage will cause multiple negative repercussions in other spheres of that child's life for years to come. No wonder Scripture warns fathers not to exasperate or provoke their children.

Like a university professor, we can make faith and spirituality much too complicated or cumbersome and much too negative or boring for the next generation.

When she was in high school, my daughter Shawna asked a huge question. "Dad, how do we know Christianity is true? How do we know one of the other religions isn't true?" I could have felt threatened by her question. Instead, I thought, *What an extraordinarily important question for a young Christ follower to ask.* That day we began a dialogue that helped Shawna make faith in Jesus Christ her own. Today, as a graduate student, she's helped stretch my own faith in positive, healthy ways.

Shawna and I always want to keep growing in our heart devotion to God. The minute I stop asking questions, wrestling with doubt, and embracing hope, I stop loving God, no matter how much I continue to learn about him.

Spiritually, wherever I was years ago isn't good enough anymore. The same is true in any sphere of life. Right before I finished college, I made a note that "the world's greatest supercomputer (designed by Seymour R. Cray of Minneapolis) has a maximum storage capacity of 77 billion bits of information." Since eight bits are the equivalent of one byte, Cray's storage capacity in 1981 was about 9.6 gigabytes, and that was in large, heavy appliance-type boxes. A generation later, lightweight laptops can easily store 160 gigabytes on a single machine.

It's almost startling how much things have changed.

When my son Jon was about nine years old, we received a heavy box from a friend. Inside, we found a bunch of metal pieces and a sixteen-page instruction manual that explained how to assemble a satellite dish. The manual included no illustrations, just straight text set in narrow columns of nine-point type. Jon took an hour to read the manual, then sat on the floor and spent the next four hours assembling the satellite dish. He took only one break, for about fifteen seconds, when he said, "Oops," unscrewed a piece, then screwed it back in correctly. When Jon was finished, the satellite dish was completely accurate, down to the tilt of the axis. Less than five years later, it was an obsolete relic.

What about the faith Jon, Shawna, and I each embraced years ago? Is it obsolete as well? That may sound like a rhetorical question, but that's not how I meant it. We all, at some time in our lives, have to wrestle with this question.

For some, the answer ends up being, "Yes, faith in Jesus Christ—at least as I understood it years ago—is inadequate or outdated." If we're not careful, however, we can end up searching for new answers intellectually—answers about God, consciously or unconsciously divorced from an authentic desire to know God himself. The results can be disastrous.

FAITH WRECKER Studying about God without heart devotion

THE DANGER OF GOING TOO FAR

In 1964, a monstrous earthquake hit Alaska. At the moment of impact, it registered 9.2 on the Richter scale—like twenty-five thousand atomic bombs going off at once. The ocean suddenly vanished around many of the Aleutian Islands in the Bering Sea off the southern and southwestern coast of Alaska. Shipwrecks, rusting six-foot-high crab pots, and sea anemones suddenly lay exposed to the sky. Then terrifying tsunami waves—thirty, sixty, and in some cases well over a hundred feet high—slammed into the islands, causing untold misery and grief.

A few months later, my father moved our family to Kodiak, the largest of those islands. My father built huge communications towers so the government could alert Alaskans of incoming tsunamis and other potential threats. Out of necessity, my dad's work took him away from home for months at a time. When he returned home, however, he often took us to explore the wonders of the island where we lived.

On one occasion, while playing on a gorgeous but isolated beach on the east end of Kodiak Island, I stumbled upon a strange round metal object about eighteen inches in diameter. More than a dozen metal rods protruded from the sphere. I grabbed several rods and pushed the object. It haphazardly rolled a little ways. I pushed again and again until I got it rolling nonstop down the beach. Suddenly I heard loud shouts. My parents rushed up and scolded me like I had never been reprimanded before. In no uncertain terms, I was told never to touch such objects again. I had been playing with a bomb that could have ripped me apart.

That undetonated explosive is a symbol of the destructive potential of religious studies without a prerequisite love for God. Such study can actually damage our faith.

Take the seemingly innocuous study of numbers. The Bible uses every number from one to fifty—except forty-three and forty-four. Some have wondered what this missing numbers mean. Did God accidentally forget them? After all, in ancient times numbers had specific meaning. We're often reminded that the number one speaks of God's unity. Some say forty represents God's testing and his judgment if we fail. But what about forty-three and forty-four?

I believe that if you wrestle with that question for any length of time, you're going to damage your soul. The numbers two, three, four, five, six, seven, twelve, and twenty-four may very well represent something. But not all numbers have meaning beyond the numeric. In this case, the more you wrestle with something God doesn't care about—a couple of missing numbers—the worse off you'll be.

Many famous agnostics and atheists, including Ernst Haeckel, David Friedrich Strauss, Charles Darwin, Ludwig Feuerbach, Karl Marx, and Friedrich Nietzsche, pursued theological studies divorced from heart devotion to God. Most of them attended universities rich in religious tradition, either Catholic or Protestant. By the time they graduated, any faith they might have had was washed away.

If the past four centuries have proved anything, it's that theological education doesn't necessarily build up one's faith. Instead, if the study of God's Word is separated from God himself, it can actually tear faith down.

On one occasion my friend Scott Larsen had the opportunity to interview best-selling author and university professor Walter Wangerin Jr. about his experiences walking away from faith in graduate school and then coming back—a different way.

> "I found out that I had no faith because my belief had always been supported by the strong structures around me," Wangerin told Scott. "It was as if they held me and made me walk when I wasn't capable of walking at all. And when the structures went away, then all gestures of faith left as well. I could not return at the level where I left, and this is the case for many people, I suspect. . . . You have to enter

at a different level. Because leaving the church is as much a part of the sequence of faith as staying with the church. The church often thinks that this person has now fallen and is out of the process altogether. What I declare is wherever that person ends up, these are stages of faith too. So my declaring that I was separate from God didn't mean I had fallen. . . . That's not backsliding; that's dramatic forward moving. It's coming to the truth that you hadn't recognized before.

"When I returned to the church, then, it did not work for me to come in at that simplistic level where all things are explained, and the things that are difficult are simply ignored."[4]

On another occasion, Scott talked with best-selling author and psychologist Larry Crabb about his experiences. Crabb told him,

When I got into graduate school, I told myself not to believe anything that would require me to dump my intellect. Several psychology professors told me that I could not be a good psychologist and still believe in nonsensical Christianity. So for a year or two I became a self-chosen agnostic. I wanted to start from scratch to see what is true.

Crabb added,

Being an orthodox Christian means allowing the truth of Christianity to be absorbed into one's soul, which changes one's approach to life. I began moving toward God, wanting to relate to him, not just to do what I was told.[5]

Before we go any further, please hear what I'm not saying. I'm not arguing against higher education. Far from it. I taught at the undergraduate level for a decade and at the graduate level for four years. I continue to serve as a guest lecturer at colleges, universities, and seminaries.

Additionally, I'm not arguing against theological or biblical studies within a faith community or on your own. I've done both for several decades. What I am saying is that whatever we do needs to be evaluated against the question, Is this helping me grow closer to God? That is, is my heart growing more in love with the true God? Am I acting more lovingly to my family, friends, coworkers, neighbors, strangers, and the needy and oppressed?

TRYING AGAIN

Of course, whatever habits, practices, and spiritual disciplines I find helpful are personal in nature. They may or may not be helpful to others. In fact, the more I insist that others (my family, friends, fellow church members, neighbors) follow in my footsteps, the more I end up harming them.

That doesn't mean that I fail to live out my faith before others, but I don't point an accusing finger and insist that they follow my example. If the fruit of my actions isn't compelling enough in and of itself, I should be quiet. The more I urge and argue and insist, even with my children, the more I'm going to drive them from the faith.

We see this clearly in the lives of the children and grandchildren of the great English evangelical reformers, as many of these descendants rejected and renounced the faith. They agonized deeply over their loss of faith and often still professed a love for Jesus, but they became agnostics or atheists instead. Part of this was the result of their parents' or grandparents' anti-intellectualism, which left them unprepared to face the tough questions and outright attacks posed by academia, but a bigger part was all the petty legalism they had grown up abhorring.[6]

Their response isn't much different from many in today's generation. One college graduate put it this way: "Raised in a world of stained glass windows and Wednesday night prayer meetings, I had been driven away by the gossip, judgmentalism, and legalism that confronted me every time I darkened the church doors. . . . I felt scorned by other Christians. So I scorned right back by refusing to be associated with my church. The irony is that I'd done to them exactly what they'd done to me."[7]

What's helpful and right for me is only that—helpful for me.

When my friend Spencer Burke served as pastor of Mariners Church near Newport Beach, California, he often had people confide that they felt burned out and dry in their spiritual lives.

His response?

"I'd ask them what they were doing when they felt that way. If it was devotions, I'd tell them to stop doing devotions for a while. If it was acts of service, I'd tell them to stop serving others for a while.

"Whatever it was that they were doing to try to get close to God, I'd tell them to do exactly the opposite.

"The weird thing is that it worked. Sometimes they returned to those expressions after they took a break and sometimes they didn't. Sometimes they found new ways of communing with God. But it was the breaking away, the giving oneself permission, that ultimately led to breakthrough."[8]

Again, whatever I think about spirituality needs to be evaluated against the question, Is this helping me grow closer to God? Sometimes that means trying something different. Of course, that's easier said than done, especially if you're a deep thinker.

I'm so glad God loves intellectuals. He's certainly not afraid of our toughest questions. We just need to know ahead of time what to do with questions we (and others) can't answer—or can't answer yet.

DEALING WITH DOUBTS

So, what do we do with questions we can't answer?

Andrea, a philosophy major at the University of Wisconsin–Madison, asked me, "If we cannot understand God fully, who are we to claim to understand anything he has told us and thereby rightly practice it or approximate rightly practicing it? Without this complete understanding, how can we ever be sure that something is of God without doubting?" Those are good questions.

Thankfully, a lack of understanding is not a valid reason for unbelief or disbelief, at least not in the natural or physical world. For many years humans believed the earth was the center of the universe—simply because no one had done the research yet to suggest otherwise.

In the realm of the natural world, not understanding why things work the way they do inevitably leads to seeking more truth—not rejecting what we already know. A majority of people are baffled when asked to explain how electricity works. How does the power of the churning water through a dam become a refined energy source that comes through wires into our homes and is controlled by simple switches? We may not understand it—but we still use it.

The same is true in the spiritual realm. As finite individuals, we certainly don't fully understand who God is, let alone how or why he designed faith and spirituality as he has. In fact, our understanding is very limited.

If life has been very painful for you, you're probably all the more aware of how little you understand.

Conversely, if life has been good, you may wonder if God is necessary.

If you've been introduced to teachings that contradict what you've believed in the past, you may feel confused.

Conversely, if you're only now coming to an understanding about faith in God, you may have no feelings toward God yet.

Asking questions, wrestling with doubt, and embracing hope

FAITH BUILDER

WHAT ABOUT FEELINGS?

Over the past generation much has been made in evangelical Christianity of the importance of a "personal relationship with God." But what if you don't feel any connection between you and God? Again, this isn't a rhetorical question.

Kevin, an acquaintance of mine, explained his dilemma to me this way:

> I used to be a rather obstinate atheist. After hearing what you and others have to say, particularly regarding postmodern atheistic belief, I have fully realized the futility and negativity of atheistic thought, a realization I was moving toward anyway, but that has finally been brought home to me. There were times when I thought I could glimpse the truth Jesus represents. By the end, however, I was left undecided and had not opened my heart to Jesus.
>
> I have been attending church for the past couple of months, and I have been uncertain about how I am supposed to respond to God; I am uncertain what feelings I am supposed to harbor. I have prayed to God to show himself to me (by this I do not mean I am testing him, only reaching out to him and hoping he will reach back). Yet I still have had no strong, clear feeling of faith.

I think the main reason for this concerns my background (largely academic), which involved high levels of critical analysis and evaluation, including much doubting of everything I was confronted with. This meant that I approached Scripture, God, and Jesus, as 'theoretical' matters to be evaluated thoroughly before I accepted them. I realized that this is what I was doing. I disliked it but felt I could not escape from this because analysis and evaluation were methods ingrained in me. It is hard for me to forget them or push them aside and focus on a spiritual level (which has been unknown to me) where I can build faith in God.

Is faith a step just taken, trustingly and acceptingly, and then built on later? If I do not have the genuine feelings I think a believer would have, then am I meant to make this step? Or would it be wrong to do so?

Basically, I am unsure about how I am supposed to respond to God and how I would initiate, and build upon, faith in him. How do I know I am not just forcing myself to have these feelings, and therefore they are not genuine?

To a degree, I understand what Kevin is saying. When I came to faith, I kept looking for some inner spark to confirm I had become a child of God. That mystical feeling eluded me for a long time. When it finally came, I had to ask myself, *Is this what it means to know God?*

Subsequently, whenever I felt I had let God down and felt disillusioned with myself, any positive spiritual feelings I might have had disappeared immediately.

The closer we've felt to God, the worse we feel when he disappears.

GREG'S STORY

My friend Greg has studied more about God than most people I know. Yet after a series of pastoral tragedies and leadership conflicts, he resigned as pastor of my church in 2002. What followed was the darkest time of doubt, depression, anger, and resentment he had ever experienced.

Greg took a job watering the Top O' Scott golf course at night. On one particularly chilly night, as he knelt down to insert a sprinkler head into the irrigation coupler, the pipe broke. A geyser of water instantly shot ten feet into the air, soaking him from head to foot. He knew he was in trouble. In a moment, the water would flood the green and ruin play for the next day. He was out of his element, out of answers, and out of patience.

"I wanted to crawl off and just go away," Greg remembers. "At that moment I was standing on more than just the fifteenth fairway of the Top O' Scott golf course. I was standing on the precipice of faith."

As Greg stood on the golf course that night, he realized he had come to a new moment of truth. As the water from that broken pipe gushed around him and a teenage coworker hurried to repair the blunder, Greg felt that he was without hope.

A couple of weeks later, he was again watering the fifteenth fairway, but this time the scene was very different. The weather had turned and summer had finally come to Portland in its majestic splendor. The moon was full and bright. However, even on this perfect night, Greg just couldn't seem to find any freedom or joy as his memory led him back to that prison cell of recrimination and bitterness.

It was then that he began to reflect on the words of the psalmist:

Why am I discouraged?
Why is my heart so sad?

I will put my hope in God!
I will praise him again—
my Savior and my God!

The psalmist was not just in a crisis of faith but in a crisis of hope—and so was Greg. Greg discovered that he needed to embrace hope, something he had ignored in the past due to his optimistic nature.

"I never understood the importance of hope in the Christian life," Greg says. "My natural bent is positive, upbeat, and optimistic. The grace of hope was something I could easily overlook. But divine hope is vital in the life of the Christian.

"God renewed my hope on that golf course. Every time I put a sprinkler head into the coupler, I would get sprayed, but it didn't matter. The water felt cool; the course was all mine. I drove my cart to the fourteenth green, looked out over the city lights, listened to the coyotes, and watched some evening swallows gliding over the open fairways.

"Tears of thanksgiving welled up in my eyes. I thanked God for that moment. I thanked him for that job that let me play golf in the day and sit alone on the course at night. And I realized I wasn't alone. He was with me on that fourteenth green, sharing the beauty of all he made: the stars, the swallows and coyotes, the breeze, the warm summer night. He had chosen that place for me to restore hope in him."

After restoring Greg's faith and hope, God opened up doors for my friend to work with the Billy Graham Evangelistic Association (BGEA) on a project called Mi Esperanza—"My Hope."

Ironically, Greg never would have considered that career change and cross-country move unless he had gone through a major crisis.

As it turned out, BGEA was looking for someone who had

been a pastor, who had worked in television broadcasting, and who had traveled in scores of countries around the world for years. Greg was their man.

As a result of Mi Esperanza, well over 9 million people have decided to follow Jesus Christ. At one point, when BGEA's board of directors convened, their conference room was filled with stacks of paper listing the names of the 2.5 million most recent inquiries. Imagine!

Out of a deep crisis, God brought an epic wave of evangelism that far eclipses anything BGEA has done in years.

I don't know what your story is. Perhaps you've had your own crisis. Perhaps you don't have answers anymore. Perhaps you've experientially lost your faith and hope in God.

The answer isn't to throw away everything you know about God and the Bible. But it also might not be found in a seminary.

Study, in and of itself, isn't the answer. Instead, no matter how you feel, the answer can be found only by walking back to God again, probably on a different route than you've taken before, possibly for a bigger purpose than you've ever had.

EVERYONE ASKS THE SAME QUESTION at some point in life. *Why me?*

When we pulled up to our house at a quarter to midnight and our oldest daughter's bedroom light was still on, we knew something was wrong. Our daughter Elizabeth, then age fourteen, could hardly wait to tell us what had happened.

"Well, you'll never guess what Benjamin did this afternoon." Gulp. Our then sixteen-month-old son certainly knew how to give us a good scare—just a few days earlier, he had horrified his mother by pulling two butcher knives out of the dishwasher and brandishing them like swords. (To say the least, we hid all the knives after that.)

"So," we asked, "what in the world did he do this time?"

"You're not going to believe it."

"Try us."

"If you don't believe me, the message is still saved on voice mail."

"What message?"

"The message the police station left right before the two squad cars screamed down the street and pulled up to the house."

I quietly reminded myself to breathe.

"And why were they in such a hurry to get here?"

"Well, Benjamin was playing with the phone. The babysitter was too tired to keep chasing Benjamin all around the house."

"And?"

"Benjamin pushed the On button, then a 9, then a 1, then another 1."

"Right."

"Like I said, I knew you weren't going to believe me."

The odds of Benjamin punching the right sequence—on his first try—are a bit staggering (20,736 to 1, in this case).

Sure enough, when we checked voice mail, there it was:

> This is 9-1-1. We received a call and I believe it may be from a small child, because I could hear babbling in the background and buttons were being pushed. If this is an actual emergency, please have an adult call back.

When no one called back, of course, they had to find out what was wrong.

When the babysitter answered the door, her jaw dropped at the sight of several policemen on our front porch, armed and ready for anything. And up toddled Mr. Diaper, phone in hand, still babbling away.

The babysitter's first thought: *Why me?*

WHEN REALITY HITS

Of course, most of the time when policemen are on your front porch, it's not the makings of a humorous story. Anything but. At one time or another, we all find ourselves—forced against our will—facing an ugly reality:

- A drunk driver kills someone you love
- A burglar ransacks your home

- A friend gossips maliciously about you
- A coworker maligns you relentlessly
- A competitor tarnishes your reputation
- A job is lost to corporate downsizing
- An abusive parent threatens you
- A spouse turns against you unexpectedly
- A rebellious child disdains you
- A child is diagnosed with leukemia
- A chronic illness produces overwhelming pain

Sometimes it feels as if the circumstances of life are going to crush us; they're simply too much to endure. When that happens, it's only natural to ask the question: *Why?*

That question has haunted entertainer Ellen DeGeneres. By the time she reached her twenties, she'd already had a hard life. Then her girlfriend was killed in a car accident shortly after they'd had a fight. Afterward, when Ellen couldn't figure out any answers, she wrote her first comedy piece, aptly titled "A Phone Call to God." In it she asks God to explain things that don't seem to make sense in this life.

The question *Why?* also haunted my friend and former professor Dr. Garry Friesen. A mysterious malady left him in constant agony. Even powerful painkillers had no effect. At his lowest ebb, he tucked into the fetal position and did not move for thirty-six hours. He felt he was losing his mind. He tried to endure in ten-minute increments. He had two goals: (1) don't curse God and (2) don't commit suicide. Not very impressive goals, but Garry will let God be the judge of his response. After all, God blessed the angry and ranting Job for his endurance and gave him a whole book in the Bible. Like Job, Garry's pain forced an ultimate question: "If we lose everything but God, is he enough?"[1]

GOD AS HE TRULY IS

The unanswered *why* question can move us either closer to God or much further away.

When we face crushing circumstances and God doesn't intervene, it's easy for our view of ourselves and our view of God to become warped.

When things start going wrong, our first instinct is to blame God. Instead of waiting to see how he is going to show himself to us through our trials, we sometimes demand that God solve our problems. When he doesn't, our mental image of God becomes smaller because we start imagining that he's just as limited as we are. Eventually, we might even threaten to bag our Christianity altogether. Ironically, that might be exactly what God wants us to do.

I've come to the conviction that God wants nothing more than for us to discard our man-made, limited concepts of who he is. We can begin to form a right view of God's greatness, goodness, and glory only after we first remove our small, misshapen ideas.

God is greater than any and every action, thought, sacrifice, or representation generated by the likes of you and me. God is also bigger than humanity collectively, including even our greatest leaders down through the ages. So surely he is bigger than any and every situation we face, even if it doesn't feel like it at the time.

According to the prophet Isaiah, God's greatness can be compared to a number of things:

God is greater than the vastness of the oceans. Scientists tell us that the earth has some 316.8 million cubic miles of water on it—in the oceans alone. That's enough to cover the entire planet with water two miles deep. Yet God can hold it all "in his hand."

God is greater than the vastness of the earth. Scientists tell us this planet has 259,875,620,000 cubic miles of land mass. We can't even imagine how tedious it would be to weigh the dirt in a small hill. Yet God knows exactly how much each mountain weighs.

God is greater than the vastness of space. Today we measure in feet and inches. In ancient times measurements were calculated using "spans." One span represented a distance of about nine inches, or about the length of one's hand. If we were to take a measuring tape and mark off the distance from here to the moon span by span, it would take us fifteen years to do it, assuming someone could mark a span every second of every minute of every hour of every day of every week of every month for every one of those fifteen years. Yet God marked off every span across the universe, some 30 billion light-years (as far as we can tell), in no time. Beyond that, he knows every star by name.

The point isn't that God is a lot smarter than I am. It's that he is so much bigger than the most crushing circumstances of life—and a lot smarter than I am!

When I finished college, we were told that computer technology was only beginning to be harnessed by science and industry. Echoing what I was hearing at the time, I wrote in my journal, "Soon all of us will have computers in our own homes to do some of our thinking for us. And we'll need them. Scholars estimate that man's knowledge, gathered and collected for thousands of years, is doubling every five to ten years. We now know more today about the ancient Greeks than the ancient Greeks knew about themselves."

Looking back, it's laughable how much things have changed since personal computers were first introduced. The amount of information I can tap into within a fraction of a second is staggering, but what is that compared to God's infinite wisdom?

If you think about it, God never learned anything. He just knows. He didn't have to go to school to find out how to make a universe. He didn't have to read a book to discover how to create the ten plagues that devastated ancient Egypt. No one had to tell God how to fix the mess we're in.

Contrary to popular rumor, none of us are ever going to offer God a better way to run our lives—no matter how hard we try.

THE CHOICE IS OURS

So what do we do when life is all screwed up and—as far as we can tell—God isn't making anything better? Do we tell God how to fix things? Do we tell God off?

Intellectually, we want to do the former. Emotionally, we want to do the latter. Volitionally, we want to do our own thing. Spiritually, we want to walk away. Yet the apostle Peter was right: Where else can we go?

One of the best foreign-language films I've ever seen is *Sophie Scholl: The Final Days*, which won a stack of awards. The main character, Sophie, is one of Germany's most famous anti-Nazi heroines. At one point in the movie, just before she is scheduled to be executed, Sophie is allowed to see her parents one last time.

"We'll meet again in eternity," Sophie says.

"Don't forget, Sophie: Jesus," her mother replies.

"Yes, Mother. But you neither."

A short time later, Sophie is beheaded.

Over the past couple of generations Sophie has been admired by her family, friends, and an entire nation. The award-winning movie about her life ensures her memory will live on for generations to come.[2]

Still, after watching the movie, I wondered, *What happened to Sophie's mother? When all was said and done, did she remember Jesus?*

If not, would you blame her? Do you believe that God really

can bring anything good out of crushing circumstances, even the unjust death of an outstanding young woman?

Experiencing the most crushing circumstances in life

FAITH WRECKER

NATHAN'S STORY

On the surface, it doesn't always appear that God brings good out of crushing circumstances.

By the time he was an adult, Nathan had attended the Church of Christ, a Methodist church, a Seventh-Day Adventist church, and a Baptist church. He was even baptized three different times, just to be sure! But when he lost his job and his financial stability, and his marriage began to fail, he found himself turning away from God.

Nathan wanted to trust that God would work things out for the best, but it was taking everything he had not to hate God outright. During the time, he sent me an e-mail:

> Now, especially, God is silent. If I think that I've ever received an answer in the past twenty-two months, it's always been "No" or "Go away." It doesn't matter how good I am or how bad I am—or how much I pray or read the Bible or just genuinely try to be a Christian . . . The situation never gets better. It's just disappointment after disappointment. Hope is now a cruel hoax . . . It's repeatedly taken away. Where is God when you really need him?

For months, Nathan kept looking for God. He couldn't pray, but he continued to e-mail me about his struggles to still believe in God.

I've tried over and over to "surrender all" to God. There's a hard ball of something inside of me that screams "Get away" at Jesus, probably because of all the junk I've dealt with in evangelical Protestant churches. It seems as though I have to give up on my personality in order to become a Christian . . . I've gone as far as I can go, reached as far as I can, made mistakes, gotten up, tried again, and carried on . . . I've tried, failed, and opened myself to God as much as I can. So where is he?

In the end Nathan moved, and our correspondence abruptly ended. How does his story end? Well, at that point, probably rather sadly. But God hasn't given up on him. Neither have I. If Nathan is like others I've corresponded with, I'll hear from him again.

IN THE FACE OF TRAGEDY

When tragedy strikes repeatedly, it's often more than most of us can bear. My friend Adjbane felt like this when his wife, Adele, died in a car accident. And the very next day, his wife's sister, who was helping take care of the children, suddenly took ill and died.

Any time two such tragedies happen so closely together, the Muslim and animist people where Adjbane lives always assume a curse. Adjbane is a Christian, so he faced intense pressure to go back to the traditional religion of his people, contact the spirits, and try to appease them by sacrifices or by taking revenge on whoever is said to have brought these tragedies upon his family.

In the aftermath, I hardly knew what to pray. What would you have told Adjbane?

At my weaker moments, Bible verses like Romans 8:31 get to me. How could Paul the apostle have the audacity to suggest that "if God is for us, who can ever be against us?" *Let me tell you, Paul!*

The shocking truth is that God loved us long before we ever loved him. Some have scoffed at the traditional interpretation of John 3:16, saying instead that God loves the world, but that doesn't include individuals.

But God's love is radically different from the "love" people naturally show to each other. The focus of his love is radically different, as well.

That God should love *us* so excited the apostle John that he wrote, "See how very much our Father loves us, for he calls us his children, and that is what we are! But the people who belong to this world don't recognize that we are God's children because they don't know him."

Still, when tragedy strikes repeatedly, as it did for my friend Adjbane, it's hard to see God's love. At that point, we can only perceive his bewildering hand that seems to be striking us again and again. I've certainly felt that way. But it isn't accurate or true.

I used to love playing Uno until my son Benjamin caught on to the game. Benjamin delights in hammering me with Wild cards, Skip cards, Reverse cards, Draw Two cards, and Draw Four cards. Near the end of the game, I'm often sitting at the table with a fistful of cards while Benjamin is counting down: three cards, two cards, Uno, game over.

When it comes to life, sometimes we think that because we're followers of Jesus Christ or because we're "good" Christians, God will remove all the Wild, Skip, Reverse, Draw Two, and Draw Four cards from the deck. That's a lie. I don't care who has told you otherwise. The Bible is very clear about this.

MARCHAUNA'S STORY

It doesn't matter how dedicated you are, how much Bible you know, how fervently you've served God. When tragedy strikes and your faith is shaken to the core, you have to decide—like Job—*Will I still worship God?*

I used to define worship as the feelings I had when listening to or singing music that exalts God. I've discovered, however, that worship can take many forms. It can take the form of singing and raising my hands to God. It can take the form of kneeling in private praise and adoration when God answers one of my heartfelt prayers. It can even take the form of quiet tears and prayers when my strongest human desires are thwarted for a time.

In the end, all of these forms of worship might even merge into something unexpected.

When my friend Marchauna learned that the baby she was carrying was dead, her heart broke. Her faith was shaken to its very core. She was left to question everything she believed about God and his goodness. When her sister died a few months later, the foundation of her faith was already cracked and broken.

Only ten days after her sister's death, Marchauna learned that she and her husband, Chris, were being relocated to Alaska. It was just one more serious aftershock following a major earthquake.

Marchauna was tired, broken, and grieving. She didn't want to go to Alaska, though they were scheduled to leave in three days. She asked Chris to pray about not going. As she sat on the couch, begging God to let her stay home, to take a break, to rest, the words of the song "Press On" by Selah came on the stereo.

"God soothed my heart and gave me the strength to press on," Marchauna recalls. "It has been a daily issue here. The schedule has been intense. Chris has been gone much of the time, and God has been pruning me severely. Yet through it all,

God has given me the strength to press on, sometimes one step at a time."

GOD BEHIND THE SCENES

The story of the most famous Joseph in all of history—the Joseph who has been featured in award-winning films, videos, and DVDs—is found in the first book of the Bible.

In Genesis 37, we find Joseph at age seventeen. I think it's safe to say that he was still a bit immature. Incredibly, Joseph received an authentic vision of God's plan for his life. Yet he was struggling in the midst of a very dysfunctional family. First, Joseph's brothers hated him. And second, while Joseph was favored by his father, for all practical purposes his father left Joseph unprotected from his brothers' hatred.

Joseph's life isn't just a story about someone who lived a long time ago. It's a story about us. All of us.

Romans 15:4 reminds us, "Such things were written in the Scriptures long ago to teach *us*. And the Scriptures give us hope and encouragement as *we* wait patiently for God's promises to be fulfilled" (emphasis added).

Joseph's story helps us see God behind the scenes, at work in and through the narrative of our lives. Because the reality is, God is always doing something bigger than you or I can see.

The great paradox of life is that suffering and humility are necessary steps to reveal God's best in us. We see that truth in Romans 5, in James 1, in 1 Peter 3:13-22, and many other Scripture passages.

The fact that God's preparation and training program includes hardships and trials is a very unpopular and countercultural message. We'd much rather enjoy a nice, comfortable lifestyle free of pain and suffering. But we might as well face reality.

When we enter the "Joseph zone," we're talking about a way of life that's much different from the one you and I live. Yet we find that God, God's principles, and life's difficulties haven't changed over time.

In Genesis 37, we don't hear God's perspective, but we can see his fingerprints everywhere.

First, we see God in the *future*. Joseph's dreams offered a picture of God's plans for the future. Of course, at that point, Joseph had no idea what his dreams really meant.

Second, God is also seen in the *past*. From Genesis chapters 1 to 36, we see God visiting Adam and Eve, visiting Abraham, and granting visions and dreams. Without question, Jacob must have relayed all those stories, life lessons, and promises of God to his sons. And almost for certain, Joseph and his brothers had been told a dark, foreboding prophecy about Abraham's descendants one day being enslaved and mistreated.

At some point on his journey to Egypt, Joseph surely realized that he was the first of Abraham's family to enter the bonds of slavery. He also must have known that the rest would follow. Thankfully, Joseph's heartbroken plea for God to save him eventually became a plea for God to save his family from a similar fate. Remarkably, God answered that prayer for many generations.

Finally, God is seen in the *present*. Joseph's knowledge of God's promises to his family in the past and the dreams he'd had of the future helped Joseph deal with the crushing circumstances of his life.

God speaks to us in many ways. Whether we read the Bible or not, God can use circumstances to bend and shape and mold and refine our character.

How do we enfold this threefold perspective into our own lives?

We do so by affirming this overarching reality: Because of God's amazing work in the *past*, I can trust God to bring *future* good for many people out of my *present* difficulties.

Seeing God as he is and believing that he is working behind the scenes

FAITH BUILDER

NINE TRUTHS

I remember the first time I read the book of Genesis and came to the Joseph story. It started out so harshly, I felt relieved when Joseph was released from slavery and prison. I couldn't believe it when he rose to power second only to Pharaoh in ancient Egypt.

To say the least, I wasn't surprised when Joseph hid his identity when his brothers came to Egypt, attempting to buy desperately needed grain for their families back in Canaan. I admit I got a certain sense of pleasure when Joseph spoke harshly to them, jerking them around.

By the time I turned the page from Genesis 44 to Genesis 45, I could sense that Joseph's revenge was right around the corner. At the climactic moment, when Joseph revealed his true identity, I expected his brothers to be slaughtered like a bunch of pigs.

Instead, Joseph forgave them.

I broke down and wept. After all they had done to him years earlier, I didn't see that coming. How could he?

Years later, looking at Joseph's life anew through an informed New Testament perspective, I find myself repeatedly affirming nine life-changing truths. Difficult as they are, you may wish to embrace them as well.

1. In this life, I will be mistreated by others.
2. Even if I am not yet reconciled with those who have hurt me, I can experience release from bitterness by trusting in God's plan for my life.

3. I can be sure that God has a good purpose when he allows me to experience difficult circumstances.

4. God isn't the one to blame.

5. God wants to test my character and cultivate my trust in him so I'll be able to walk alongside and encourage others.

6. To be reconciled with those who have hurt me, I often must take the risk of revealing my heart—both my pain and my love.

7. To be reconciled, I often must invite those people to draw close to me and speak freely with me.

8. Reconciliation isn't always possible, but my responsibility is to do as much as possible to live at peace with others.

9. If someone has something against me, even if that person hates me and even if I've done nothing wrong, I need to go to him or her and do all that I can to be reconciled.

"Do all that I can" is a biblical concept (Romans 12:18) that lets us know God is the ultimate realist. He knows that life on earth isn't heaven. It can be hellish.

Thankfully, Joseph's story doesn't end in tragedy—and ours doesn't have to either.

ANNA'S STORY

Just as difficult as losing a child is losing a parent while you are still young.

Shortly after I began serving as an adjunct professor at one of the top comprehensive undergraduate colleges in the western United States, I met a talented journalism student named Anna Harrell. In time, she told me how her faith had almost been crushed by the tragic loss of her mother.

The spring that Anna turned fourteen, her mom was diagnosed

with cancer. After months of declining health, her mom could no longer make it to the bathroom on her own. Anna's dad brought in a mechanical hospital bed because she couldn't lie down comfortably anymore. Her once perfectly styled brown hair hung limp and gray.

But she still called Anna and her brothers and sisters into her room every day for prayer and Bible study. She could no longer read the words herself, but she thrilled to hear them. And though pain racked her body, she praised God for his goodness to her. Anna never heard her mom complain or question the purpose of her illness. As her physical strength waned, her faith actually seemed to grow.

One evening, Anna's mother called each of her kids into her bedroom. When it was Anna's turn, Anna struggled to fight back tears.

"You don't have to cry," her mother said. "It's okay. God will take care of you." She wiped Anna's tears with her hand. "Anna, my sunshine girl," she began. "You have such a good heart. Continue to seek God in all you do." Her voice weakened to a near whisper. Every night Anna prayed that God would heal her mom. She often dreamed that her mom's illness was only a nightmare, only to awaken on a soggy pillow and realize she was living the nightmare.

She would have given anything to wake up from the nightmare the day her dad came in and said, "She's gone."

Anna had known for months that her mom's death was inevitable, but she had hoped and prayed for a miracle. Instead, she was left with only pain and questions. *How could God, being loving and kind, let Mom suffer so much? How could he let her die, leaving me with more pain than I can bear? How could he take away my mom?*

Although Anna had been a Christian since she was nine, she still needed her mom to help her understand the Bible and to encourage her to pray. She wasn't ready to be an adult, to solve problems on her own. She begged God for an answer. "I wanted to trust his judgment, to understand his plan," Anna recalls. "I didn't want to become bitter at him, but it was hard to love him when he had allowed me to hurt so much."

After the funeral, her mom's favorite hymn, "Come and Dine," played continuously in Anna's mind. She imagined her mom in heaven, singing in her new soprano voice. She pictured her mom at the banquet table in heaven, sitting with Jesus. It was then that she realized that God *had* answered her prayers. Not only had he healed her mom's cancer, he had also given her a new body that would never again feel pain. God had healed her in his own way—the best way.

"I knew God had done what was best for Mom, but was it really best for me?" Anna asked. "But I doubted that I hurt more than Mom had. And if God could take away the pain that destroyed her body, surely he could ease the pain that troubled my heart. In my desperation, I asked God to hold me and make it better, to wrap his arms around me, to speak comfort to me."

One night Anna read Isaiah 61:1-3, about how God would send Jesus to "comfort the brokenhearted . . . give a crown of beauty for ashes, a joyous blessing instead of mourning, festive praise instead of despair." She asked God to turn the pain in her heart to beauty, to turn her grief to joy. Over time, God showed Anna how to find him through studying his Word and praying.

It felt good to trust God again! It felt good to turn to someone greater than herself. In the end, Anna realized that, even in her trials, God is always trustworthy.

Until we get to the end of the story God is writing, it isn't always possible to see how good could possibly come from the losses, grief, pain, and schisms of this life.

But even in the most crushing circumstances, we can choose to trust God, see him as he is, and believe he's working behind the scenes of our lives for his glory and our ultimate good.

EIGHT

MAKING EXCEPTIONS

EVERYONE LIKES to break the rules.

Either I think there are no consequences—or, if there are, for some reason I believe I can defy the odds.

It's amazing—in this day of phenomenal technological advances, with knowledge exploding at an ever-increasing rate—that you and I can so easily ignore the obvious, the known, the true. Common sense is often gladly laid aside in favor of the latest thrill.

Reality, however, has a good way of slapping us in the face for ignoring what we know to be true.

My family enjoys going to the Oregon coast whenever we can. Most people know there are a few rules when it comes to spending time at the beach.

One rule of thumb is to think twice before you drive your car on the beach. You have to ask yourself, *Am I prepared to accept the fact that the salt in the sand and in the water is going to rust out my car if I'm not careful? And that I could lose my car if it gets stuck in the sand just about the same time the tide decides to start coming in? It's happened to others, after all. Who says it couldn't happen to me?*

The second rule is to think twice before going out into the surf.

That isn't much of a temptation in the state where I live, since the water is cold 365 days a year. But even if you can stand the cold, there's the undertow or riptide to contend with. Each year a handful of people remember too late that you can't fight an outgoing tide. The ocean's too big, too powerful. It wins almost every time. I've read the reports. I've come on the scene of several fatalities. I know it could happen to me.

The third rule you don't usually read about in the papers is still true: Think twice before picking up a piece of long, heavy, dead, brown seaweed.

Kelp litters the beaches no matter what time of year it is. It stinks, of course, but for some unknown reason, some people have a compulsive need to pick up the stuff and snap it in the air like a whip. Now if you've ever talked with someone who's actually done that, you would know better.

Still, running along the beach with Renée and the kids, I found a thirty-foot piece of brown seaweed and impulsively picked it up. *I'm not going to be a fool and whip this kelp sideways,* I told myself. *This seaweed's going to snap in the air over my head.*

"Watch this, kids," I yelled. *Swoosh!* Sure enough, that mighty piece of kelp went whistling through the air. And in all my life I've never been hit so hard in the face.

As I said before, reality has a good way of getting our attention if we ignore what we know to be true. It doesn't matter how old we are, how rich we are, how many years we've spent in school, how fancy our computers are. Reality doesn't make exceptions.

We all know seat belts save lives. Still, thousands of people drive without them, despite the fact that at least one out of every three people killed in auto accidents last year would have lived—if they had buckled up. It's not enough to *know* something. We have to *act* on what we know to be true.

Every twenty-one seconds, someone somewhere in America

calls 9-1-1 to report a fire. That's more than 1.5 million fires a year. More than twenty thousand people are injured in those fires, and some three thousand people actually die—mostly children killed in house fires.

The tragedy is that most families haven't developed a thought-out fire escape plan and explained it to their children. Even more tragic is the fact that a simple, portable home fire extinguisher could put out nearly 95 percent of all home fires. Yet only four out of five homes have a fire extinguisher—and, even worse, only about half of those homes' fire extinguishers still work.

Reality is reality. After I heard those statistics, I had a knot in my stomach. Renée and I had an escape plan in case of fire. Our kids knew right where to go and meet us. And of course we had a fire extinguisher in the kitchen to use if a fire ever did break out while we were awake. But for years I had never used it.

The needle on my home fire extinguisher had said "175 units of pressure" long before we ever moved into the house. I decided to test it, so I took it outside, pulled the pin, and squeezed the handle. I was ready to blast away—but all I got was one little wimpy *poof* of white dust. Not even enough to put out the candles on an average birthday cake.

For years I had been depending on an old fire extinguisher that absolutely, completely did not work.

What if a fire *had* broken out in our home before I tested my fire extinguisher and then spent twenty-two dollars to replace it? Virtually all home fires start out the same—small. Our home likely would have been engulfed in flames—all for lack of a fire extinguisher that worked.

But reality is reality. There was no point pushing reality out of sight. Once I knew the facts, I *acted* on that knowledge. Too much was at stake if I didn't. The same is true in every sphere of life, including sexuality.

Of course, life throws enough curves that it's not always possible to predict what we're going to do or say ahead of time.

FAITH WRECKER

Giving myself permission to do as I please—especially sexually—pushing reality (and God) out of sight

REPEATED CYCLES

One day on a short flight to Phoenix, the young couple next to me pulled out a portable DVD player and started watching a movie. All started out well. Then, without warning, the main character was attacked by a violent rapist. I quickly averted my eyes and winced.

Still, the first three or four seconds of that scene kept replaying in my mind. I felt violated, defiled, unclean.

Sometimes I feel the same way when I read Scripture. Maybe you have too.

I'm certainly never glad when I turn the page in my Bible and find myself staring at the book of Judges. Don't get me wrong. I've read through Judges many times. I've studied it in-depth. But there's no painting a happy face on the book. It's earthy, graphic, shocking, and utterly depressing. There is so much sin and so little evidence of people embracing God's mercy and grace.

It wasn't until days of intensive study that I finally realized the problem really isn't the depressing cycles through the book of Judges. We all go through the same cycles of sin, oppression, prayer, and deliverance. Every day. Or at least we should.

The problem isn't the *existence* of cycles of sin, oppression, prayer, and deliverance. We can't avoid them this side of heaven. The problem is the *breakdown* of those cycles.

The minute we sweep sin under the rug, the moment we try to tuck it away in a corner, the second we try to hide it from God and others, we immediately magnify the stranglehold of spiritual and moral oppression, and immediately intensify the consequences of our sins.

And that's exactly what we find in the middle of the book of Judges, chapter 13. The first verse says, "Again the Israelites did evil in the LORD's sight, so the LORD handed them over to the Philistines, who oppressed them for forty years."

Here, for the final time in the book of Judges, we find recorded the repetitive cycle of the Israelites' sin and oppression. But this time, the Israelites don't cry out to God. For forty years they just keep on sinning and paying heavier and heavier consequences.

No graphic sins are specifically mentioned here. If you read this first verse too quickly, in fact, you'd think that the thirteenth chapter of Judges is a pleasant story about the angel of the Lord announcing the birth of Samson, Israel's next great judge. It's the only section in the whole book of Judges that we could truly rate "G" for general audiences.

But in reality, the very worst sins are written all over this first verse.

Why? Because the Israelites had sunk so low they were now doing their own thing without any conscience toward God. For all practical purposes, they were atheists, independent moral agents trying to deny the reality of God.

As a result of such disbelief in God, the Israelites were slowly but surely getting pulled into the Philistine culture, both morally and spiritually. In fact, the Israelites were jubilant to be "free" of God's law so they could be a law unto themselves. Not only did they not have a judge, they didn't even want one. And when a judge finally did come on the scene, they rejected him.

Compromise was the rule of the day. It was every man and

woman doing what was right in his or her own eyes. Even when it didn't make sense. Even when it didn't work. Even when the guilt and oppression and depression had them by the necks, they were gutsy enough to say, "You only go around once. You've got to take some risks. I'll try anything once. Isn't this the life?"

God couldn't have been further from their hearts and minds. So even though life got worse and worse, for forty long years they stubbornly refused to cry out to God for help.

The fact is, if God hadn't stepped into the picture, this cycle of oppression in Judges 13 would have been Israel's last.

In 2 Chronicles 7:14, God says, "If my people who are called by my name will humble themselves and pray and seek my face and turn from their wicked ways, I will hear from heaven and will forgive their sins and restore their land."

But 2 Chronicles 7:20 says, in effect, "If my people *won't* humble themselves and won't pray and won't seek my face and won't turn from their wicked ways, then I will cause them to be oppressed to their dying day."

That was exactly the plight of the Israelites. For forty years, they refused to cry out to God. Within another forty years, if God hadn't stepped in, there wouldn't have been a nation of Israel. Most of our Bible never would have been written. The Messiah never would have come. Jesus never would have died on the cross for our sins and risen again to give us new, eternal life.

There wouldn't be any such thing as Christmas or Resurrection Sunday or the Good News that God loved the world so much that he gave his one and only Son, so that everyone who believes in him will not perish but have eternal life.

In many ways, Judges 13:1 is the scariest verse in the whole book of Judges. It's the first time that the people of Israel blatantly refused to turn back to God.

Thank God, he didn't turn his back on them.

No matter how bad things get, no matter how stubborn and sinful we become, God always extends his grace and mercy and forgiveness to us.

In the midst of the darkest period in Israel's history, the Lord came to earth to tell a childless couple that they would have a son who would begin to deliver Israel from the hands of the Philistines. It wasn't until Samson became a man, of course, that God began the job. And it took Samuel and then David many more years to finish the job. But God refused to allow the Israelites to be obliterated as a nation.

If there's one key message outside of verse 1 in this chapter, it's that God is never in a hurry to deliver us from the consequences of our sin. God knew exactly what was at stake here. He knew precisely how precarious Israel's situation was. But he also knew he was completely in control of their destiny. There was nothing the Philistines could do to thwart God's plans. You certainly don't get the picture of God rushing about, trying to fix everything in a minute.

We always need to keep in mind that God's sense of timing is often much different from ours. After all, faith is a refusal to panic.

The question often comes up: After Adam and Eve sinned in the Garden of Eden, why did God wait so many hundreds of centuries to send Jesus Christ to be our Savior?

Galatians 4:4 assures us that "when the right time came," God sent his Son, born of a woman, subject to the law, to redeem us and give us the right to be called children of God.

Why two thousand years ago? Why not three thousand years ago when the nation of Israel was in peril of being absorbed by the Philistines?

Because in God's wisdom, it wasn't the right time yet.

Think about this—if Jesus had been born fifty years earlier

or fifty years later, it would have been impossible for him to do what he did. At just the right time, when the Roman government and highway system, the Greek language, and the Jewish religious system were all in place, Jesus Christ came. A generation after his death, the Jewish nation was destroyed. Later, the Greek language lost its prominence as the language everyone spoke. And then the Roman Empire began to crumble. In his wisdom, God orchestrated Christmas and Calvary at just the right time.

Let's go back to Judges for a minute. In order to announce Samson's birth, the Lord Jesus came to earth in the form of a man. Somehow he looked like more than a man of God to Manoah and his wife. Halo? No. Glow? Possibly. Authority? Definitely.

Why didn't Jesus come two thousand years ago in this same form instead of as a helpless baby? Why Christmas? Why didn't he simply appear out of nowhere as a man? Because the Lord chose not just to *appear* but to take on humanity. In his wisdom, he knew it was the only way to rescue us.

What about God's solutions to the problems in our individual families, in our churches, in our cities, in our nation? Our problems don't just spring up. They're the result of months, years, even decades of sin, disobedience, frustration, and neglect. When we finally realize how bad things are, we can't change everything overnight. Nor should we secretly wish we could change things that fast.

God isn't the author of chaos and confusion. While he calls us to be people of action, there's a time and place for everything. We need to be cautious not to get ahead of God.

Too often, we greatly overestimate what we can do in a few months and greatly underestimate what, by God's enabling, we can do over the next few years. Including writing a vibrant new script for our lives.

The first step is coming to our senses about the junk in our lives.

Somehow, we have to abandon the ludicrous notion that no matter how bad it gets, we'll never have to truly face the consequences of our sins if we keep them quiet.

The quieter I keep my sins, the more they kill my heart. And the further I push reality (and God) out of sight.

It's not a mark of spiritual maturity to pretend we don't need God's mercy and grace. We need both every day, without exception.

TRYING TO SCRIPT LIFE

After arriving home from the airport after a whirlwind business trip, I was sitting in my favorite chair in our living room talking with my wife. I stopped abruptly when I realized that the most expensive piece of glass in our house—the living room window—had a gaping hole in the middle. I jumped from my seat.

There was no need to interview our three older children. I walked to our youngest son's bedroom and invited Benjamin to walk back with me to the living room. Then I knelt down so I was eye level with Ben, pointed toward the hole in the living room window, and calmly asked him what had happened. Ben proceeded to tell me that he had been swinging a toy airplane by a string, lost his grip, and watched it sail through the window.

While still kneeling, I grabbed Ben's right hand in mine and started shaking it proudly. He looked at me, puzzled. "Congratulations, Ben! You've done something your older sisters and older brother never did. You broke a window. And not just any window—the biggest one in the house." I continued shaking Ben's hand. He had a worried look on his face, so I continued.

"Do you think your dad ever broke a window?" Ben smiled and his shoulders immediately relaxed. Ah, yes. He remembered the stories of my childhood and youth. Life was good again.

"That's right, Ben. I broke three windows as a kid. And guess what? Your mom broke two windows and a sliding glass door. Welcome to the club!"

What was I doing? I wanted Ben to have a vivid picture of what mercy means so he could later begin to understand what's so astonishing about God's mercy, forgiveness, love, and grace.

Some time later, Renée and I were in the process of trying to adopt a four-year-old daughter who could grow up with Ben (who was born nine years after our older son). At one point, a social worker visited our home. Because her inspection was a daunting hurdle we had to clear before we could continue the adoption process, I made it a point to explain to Ben how important it was to behave properly while she was in our home.

During the social worker's visit, Ben walked through the house with us, bouncing a small ball and peppering our visitor with question after question. All attempts to quiet him proved futile. Finally, I asked Ben to take his bouncy ball and go play in his bedroom, which he did right away. He knew what was on the line.

A couple of minutes later, we heard a tremendous crash. Racing up the stairs, I looked out the back door and could see glass strewn across the patio for six feet. I ran to Ben's bedroom, where he stood crying. Glass was sprayed across the floor. I knelt down and hugged Ben.

"Dad," he cried, "I did just what you told me. I was playing with the bouncy ball and all of a sudden my window blew up." He wept harder. Instinctively, I grasped his hand and started shaking it. "Congratulations, Ben! Don't you remember how many windows your mom and dad broke as kids? But I never was able to get a window to blow out both ways." Still, in Ben's mind, it was all over, and he buried his head in my shoulder, sobbing.

I must have knelt there for four or five minutes consoling Ben. "It's going to be okay," I said. Behind me, the social worker spoke up, briefly startling me. She had followed me upstairs and watched everything.

"Yes, everything's going to be fine," she said. "You're approved."

In hindsight, I had scripted that episode. I just didn't know it at the time.

GOD OF THE SECOND CHANCE

Human fathers can show mercy if we simply stop long enough to recall our own childhood and youth. Our heavenly Father, on the other hand, shows us mercy because he remembers that we are but dust and that his one and only Son paid the penalty for our sins—including our attempts to make reality conform to our less-than-divine wants and desires.

Thankfully, we don't have to worry about God's script. The story of the Prodigal Son in Luke 15 is a vivid picture of his carefully scripted plan for welcoming us, honoring us, cherishing us, and demonstrating his love toward us. The only script we need to worry about is our own.

In Jesus' famous story, the rebel younger son was anything but respectful or submissive to his wealthy and highly revered Jewish father.

In fact, at one point, the younger son as much as says, "I can't believe it. I can't keep waiting around for you to finally keel over dead so I can inherit my half of the estate. Unless you want me to bring down your gray hairs to the grave, I demand my half *now*! Do what I say or you'll regret it!"

The first time I read this story, I had no idea how the Jewish father would respond. Would he disown his son, order his servants to forcibly throw the rebel out of the mansion, and declare him dead to the family? Historically, in many cultures around the world and down through the centuries, that's what would be expected. In fact, such high-handed, insulting, and shameful behavior sometimes called for the death penalty. It certainly would not be tolerated in any decent society.

Instead, the Jewish father gave in to his son's shocking demands. Even when someone explained to me that the Jewish father is a picture of our heavenly Father, the story still didn't make sense. The father did *what*? And *what*?

> While he [the lost son] was still a long way off, his
> father saw him coming. Filled with love and compassion,
> he ran to his son, embraced him, and kissed him.
>
> *Luke 15:20*

No wealthy, respected gentleman of that time would ever long for such a notoriously shameful son to come back home. It was completely unheard of. Such a son was considered dead, forgotten as if he had never been born, and perhaps even stricken from the genealogies. Yet not only did the Jewish father long for his son to come home, he also kept watch for him. And when the son finally did return home, the father did something else unheard of in ancient times. He tied up his long robes and *ran*. He embraced his son publicly. He kissed him. He ordered his panic-stricken servants to give his son a gold ring and fine clothes and a fabulous banquet.

What? All this for a royal military officer who returned to visit his aged father and bring honor to the family? No, not even the best son could command such a response from a father. Instead, the father offered an extravagant, embarrassing display of affection and respect for a filthy no-name pig herder nobody was supposed to acknowledge even existed, let alone admit was related to the family.

It's scandalous, to be sure. But what provoked such a response? First, the son came back to his senses, just as the father expected.

Second, the son came back home, just as the father hoped. Third, the son came back repentant, just as God knew would be the case.

Even when we don't believe in God, he believes in us. He can't wait for the day we stop pushing reality out of sight, rediscover his ideal, and allow him to write a vibrant new script for our lives. Yes, God expects a miracle. And he can't wait to throw a party in our honor—no matter what we've done.

None of this would have happened for the rebel younger son, however, if he hadn't faced the reality of his sin. As a result of doing as he pleased, he found himself far from his father, his family, and God. But then he realized they hadn't really disappeared. When he had tried to write his own script, he only messed everything up. But then he needed to write a new script in order to simply survive. It wasn't a Hollywood script, to be sure. But it was a dramatic script nonetheless.

> Father, I have sinned against both heaven and you, and I
> am no longer worthy of being called your son.   *Luke 15:21*

Other ways to say it were probably running through his head as well. "Father, I have sinned against God and brought great dishonor to your name. I acknowledge that I am no longer worthy to be called your son. I'm as good as dead to you. But please hire me on as one of your servants."

Or possibly "Father, I cursed God and disappeared from your life. All this time, you have had no idea if I was even alive. I squandered my half of the estate and am worse than swine. Please, don't curse me. Instead, please let me serve you the rest of my days. That's all I humbly ask, my lord and master."

The son must have rehearsed that script a hundred ways during his long journey home from what Scripture calls "a distant land."

More important, he had scripted his actions: I will return home. I will tell my father. . . . I will serve him humbly the rest of my life. Not words alone. Not actions alone. After all, actions speak loudest *with* words.

The apostle Peter—impetuous, bumbling Peter—recalled this amazing Jesus story many times after his master departed for heaven. It's not surprising, then, that Peter talks about writing scripts for what we're to say (see 1 Peter 3:15) and not say (see 1 Peter 3:1, 9-10) in difficult circumstances.

Believe me, Peter was a realist. He understood that life can become unbearably difficult at times. In such times, we may need someone else's help to know what script to write next.

Even more important, we need to know what scripts God will *allow* us to write.

Have you broken half of the Ten Commandments?

Do you want to break the other half?

At what point does our heavenly Father say, "That's it! There's no hope for you now. Until the day you die, you're toast."

Or is it true that God always gives us another chance?

FAITH BUILDER

Rediscovering God's ideal and allowing him to write a vibrant new script for your life

REDISCOVERING GOD'S IDEAL

Does God let anyone write a vibrant new script for life, regardless of the sin?

For several of my friends, losing their marriage has become inseparable from losing their faith. But as many others have proved, that doesn't have to be the case.

One friend, Pam Leone, resigned herself to spiritual last place after a tough divorce. In her mind, marital failure had shattered her life and rewritten her future.

Pam had always assumed that since she had married a Christian and was getting her bachelor's degree in Bible and theology, she was assured of a Spirit-filled, happy, and successful life. She and her husband, Michael, were Young Life leaders and Sunday school teachers.

Sadly, though, Pam found that her complacency caused her to become careless—in both her relationship with God and with her husband. She recalls, "My pride caused me to believe that as a Christian wife, I should not be struggling with such things as anger toward my husband. Feelings of frustration were to be squelched because 'a godly woman wouldn't feel this way!' I was constantly beating myself up for my feelings. This was a breeding ground for the anger and hard-heartedness that took hold of me."

About a year after she graduated from Bible college, Pam and Michael's marriage was falling apart. They separated and eventually filed for a divorce. After the divorce was final, Pam realized she needed to put her strong will aside and ask for God the Father's forgiveness. "He did break me and I was transformed. I totally yielded myself to his Spirit," she says.

Five years later, Pam and Michael came together with a Christian counselor to work through the issues that had driven their relationship apart. They prayed about what God would have them do with their relationship. The counselor gave them hope that God could write a new script.

"We were both scared but knew God was in control," Pam says. "Our decision to do this was based on a commitment to God." For a year, they fought, cried, and laughed as they worked hard to understand each other again and to communicate honestly.

As their reconciliation continued to bring them closer, Pam and Michael decided to get married—again! Ten months later, God blessed them with the most precious of wedding gifts—a beautiful baby girl, Rachael Elizabeth. It was as if God said, "This is my gift to you for obeying me."

"I look at our marriage as a living testament of God's grace," Pam says. "It is a gift that neither of us deserved. Sin destroyed our marriage, but God, in his mighty love for us, resurrected it through his power. It's amazing!"

STARTING OVER

Does God let anyone write a positive new script after divorce and remarriage?

Again, the answer is yes. Not because we deserve it. But because God can't wait to welcome us back.

One of my friends, Harold, had a marriage filled with infidelity, abandonment, heartache, and despair. When it finally ended in divorce, he turned to one relationship after another, looking for a way to fill the void in his life. He still believed in God; he even prayed and tried to convince God that a relationship with a non-Christian woman would be okay for him. But he couldn't shake an uneasy feeling.

"I can remember on several occasions a tugging at my heart, a calling to return to things I once knew—to my first love," Harold told me. "But I couldn't. I felt embarrassed and ashamed. But the Lord was patient. I see now as I look back that he never left me, that his hand was guiding me through the darkness."

God led Harold to the woman to whom he is now married. God was drawing her to himself as well. Through that relationship, they both discovered a new love for the Lord.

"Part of me thought that God would be angry with me," Harold said. "So much so that he wouldn't want anything to do with me. I know now that that was wrong. It was a lie. I had hurt him deeply; and, yes, I had disappointed him greatly. I had been given a precious gift and threw it away. But thankfully, his love is undying and overcomes all adversity. His love *truly* endures forever!"

REBUILDING TRUST

Does God let anyone write a vibrant new script after committing adultery?

It might seem heretical, or at least morally outrageous, but again the answer is yes.

One of my friends, John Paul, can testify to that. His affair nearly destroyed his family, but he rose to the daunting task of putting his marriage back together. For him, healing began at his church. John and his wife asked numerous Christian friends to uphold them in prayer. They also sought professional counseling and spent many hours together reading, talking, and crying.

John's job gave him the entire summer off, and during that time he spent nearly twenty-four hours a day with his wife. He rarely went anywhere, and when he did, he carried a cell phone and made sure he was with someone who could verify where he was. Although it was extremely difficult, it was also wonderfully healing.

In time, God provided a new job for John that allowed him to move away from the other woman. He and his wife renewed their vows in Maui, promising once again to remain faithful to each other.

IS IT TOO LATE?

Does God let anyone write a positive new script after multiple sexual affairs?

A while back, I received a letter from Ashley, a young woman in her early twenties who felt as if God had disappeared.

Ashley had grown up in the church and even worked at a Christian bookstore where she was surrounded by Christians—yet she felt as cold as ice. She was sexually involved with several older men, constantly looking for that "right person" to give her the love and companionship she felt she was lacking.

"I hear people talk about how God has changed their lives, but even though I accepted him, I don't see any change and I feel like God has dumped me," Ashley wrote to me in an e-mail. She explained that she had never really felt God's love or forgiveness, but she desperately wanted to.

In my reply, I told Ashley, "God knows about and completely understands your struggles. He forgives and purifies us from any and every sin we've ever committed. Believe me, Ashley, I'm not taking your situation lightly. But you haven't committed the unforgivable sin." I encouraged her to read several passages of Scripture and sent her an article about experiencing God's forgiveness.

Ashley's response was encouraging. "Last night I read some of the verses, and it was like they were talking to me." Over the next several weeks, she began to dig deeper into God's Word and found a mentor to help keep her accountable.

Then some unexpected trials hit. Ashley's ex-boyfriend called to say he wanted to get back together, but when she went to meet him, it became apparent that he was interested only in sex. She boldly refused, and he dumped her. Later that week, Ashley's mom lost her job, and someone tried to steal Ashley's car.

It was difficult to find the words to say. I told her, "Although it feels like your life is falling apart, keep reminding yourself of what is true: God is still God, he loves you, he will walk you through this difficult time to better days and a new life filled with his love, joy, strength, and peace. Only later will you really understand what God wants you to learn through this difficult time, how he wants you to trust him."

Over the following months, Renée and I both prayed for Ashley and continued to correspond with her by e-mail. We praised God at one of her responses. "It is still a time of struggling emotionally, but I am getting much better, and I'm growing much stronger. I have learned to lean only on God, because when I tried to lean on people, I just ended up hurt."

A few months later, we were even more encouraged to hear she had found a ministry position in her church, was going back to school, and had earned a promotion at her job. She wrote, "I am doing great, thanks to God. It is unbelievable how things went from really bad to really good. I have been really blessed these last weeks. I'm praying that those blessings keep on coming the way they have been and that the storm is finally over. It is in fact true that if we seek his Kingdom first, everything else will be added on."

Ashley's story is a powerful reminder to me that God doesn't give up on you and me, even if we fail him repeatedly.

No matter how much you've pushed reality aside, how long you've done as you pleased, and how hard you've tried to push God out of your life, he hasn't given up on you.

God is still watching, still eager to welcome you back, and still ready to write a vibrant new script for your life.

ANYONE CAN HAVE A BAD CHURCH EXPERIENCE. Just ask Colleen and Eric.

At first, Colleen and Eric felt great about the church they attended. After all, that's where they had met, were married, and had started raising their family.

At that point in their lives, Colleen and Eric weren't really searching for God—just the acceptance of a group of peers. So when they started noticing the church leadership's apparent contradictions and deception, they kept quiet. For several years, what they didn't know was that their church was part of a now-discredited cult.

After Colleen and Eric left the cult, they were plagued with pain, guilt, and doubt. The experience "caused me to question my own ability to see the truth," Colleen says. "I had guilt for seeing red flags along the way but not doing anything about it. You ask God for forgiveness and he gives it, but it's hard to forgive yourself. I felt cheated, like I had wasted all those years."

Despite the guilt that Colleen felt from being in a cult, to this day she wouldn't change her past. Why? God has allowed her to share her story with and assist others who have had bad church experiences.

IT COULD HAPPEN TO YOU

You don't have to join a cult to have a bad church experience.

Approximately 31 million American adults say they are Christians who have quit going to church, often because of struggles with faith or relational issues. They avoid other Christians. Yet many say their commitment to Jesus Christ is still important to them.

Tens of thousands more will join their ranks this month.

Local churches can be a safe place, a second home, for many people.

Sadly, churches also can be the setting for some of the harshest attacks against our faith.

If anyone has ever been rejected, humiliated, and hurt by the church, it's my friend Bill and his family.

When Bill was a teenager, his family joined with a few other families to start a new church. They met with a bishop from the denomination who agreed to assist with the small church plant.

Most Sundays there were only about twenty people in attendance. Bill and his two brothers assisted with candle lighting and singing in the choir, his mother played the organ, and his father read a sermon from the bishop each week.

One of the members of the congregation, Mr. Long, had always been very vocal about his desire to change the direction the church was going. After many months of behind-the-scenes politicking, Mr. Long didn't sense that things were going to go his way, so he decided to take matters into his own hands.

One morning the bishop made a surprise visit—but not to worship. He had heard "credible reports" from Mr. Long that Bill's parents were pillaging the church and playing fast and loose with the tithed money, and that they had already stolen the only really valuable piece of church paraphernalia: the silver offering plate.

Bill's dad was crushed at the accusations, but he calmly took the bishop into the church's rented office space. He opened the single-column financial ledger and showed the bishop the debits and credits—all perfectly in order. Then he took the bishop to the cupboard that held the coffee creamer, the communion wafers in an old pickle jar, and the silver offering plate.

He asked the bishop if he was fully satisfied. But by the time the bishop nodded affirmatively, it was already too late. Bill's proud Southern parents loaded the family up in their station wagon and drove away. For them, it was a massive Judas kiss— not so much from Mr. Long but from their friend and mentor, the bishop. It was two decades before Bill's parents attended a church again.

Being wounded in or by the church

FAITH WRECKER

GOD'S THIRD GREAT HUMILIATION

It's no wonder many best-selling authors over the past century have decried the sins of the church. Dorothy Sayers called them God's third great humiliation, after the Incarnation (Christmas) and the Cross (Good Friday).

It's a humiliation we cringe to even think about. But if we've had anything to do with the church in the past, we mostly cringe for our own reputation. We'd rather erase the past. But even if we could, there are plenty of present atrocities to be blamed on the church.

Thankfully, the sins of the church have nothing to do with Jesus Christ, who did anything but abuse power, let alone advocate persecution, torture, inquisitions, and warfare. Just the opposite. He could have started a horrific crusade within the hour. Instead, he submitted to mockery, beatings, flogging, and crucifixion. While hanging from the cross, he demonstrated the full extent of his love, going as far as to forgive his executioners.

The problem with the church isn't God. It is church leaders and members and pretenders who wound others, rejecting the words and wisdom and warnings of God's modern prophets. It is corrupt human beings who thwart true spirituality for selfish or sociopolitical purposes.

If anyone demonstrated how to convert politics for the good of humanity, it was renowned British statesman William Wilberforce, who led the tireless fight against slavery two centuries ago.

Wilberforce's words are worth heeding today: "Just as we would not discard liberty because people abuse it, nor patriotism, nor courage, nor reason, speech, and memory—though all abused—no more should we eliminate true religion because self-seekers have perverted it."

ROSS'S STORY

If a person has been deeply hurt by someone in the church, it can be incredibly hard for that person to love God, let alone forgive the church. I discovered this while riding one of Portland's sleek light-rail trains.

After taking a seat, I opened my satchel and pulled out my devotional Bible and a blue pen. I turned to my bookmarked page, 2 Chronicles 7, which talks about how Solomon's Temple was designed to glorify the God of heaven. I underlined several phrases about honoring the Lord's name.

Just then, the young man sitting near me interrupted my thoughts. "What are you reading?" he asked.

"The Bible," I replied.

"How come?"

"Well, I try to read the Bible every day," I said.

"That's cool," he replied. The inquisitive young man smiled.

He was dressed in a green Nike T-shirt, camouflage pants, a backward-facing baseball cap, and three-day-old stubble. "What are you reading about now?" he asked.

"I'm in 2 Chronicles," I replied. "I'm reading about Solomon's reign."

"Is that the dude who turned to witchcraft at the end of his life?"

"No, that was King Saul, the first king of Israel."

Immediately I recalled my interview that morning with Dr. Leonard Sweet, distinguished professor of evangelism at Drew University. Dr. Sweet has written several best-selling books on reaching today's postmodern youth and young adults. *Don't try to correct the errors of today's postmoderns,* he had told me. *Never criticize them. Instead, just listen. God's already at work in their lives. It's important to hear their story first.*

Despite my unneeded correction, my new friend wasn't deterred: "You know, I like reading the Bible too. My favorite part is Ecclesiasticals."

"Oh?" I replied, with a slight smile on my face over his interesting pronunciation.

At that point, my new friend—Ross, I learned later—went into a brilliant almost ten-minute exposition of the central themes of Ecclesiastes. "I still haven't figured out who wrote Ecclesiasticals, but he was a great king who reigned after David," he told me. Ross quoted several passages almost verbatim as he continued his exposition. I was impressed! And I could tell many of our fellow passengers were listening in on our conversation as well. Inwardly, I laughed. *This guy must be a Bible college sophomore in disguise.*

"Wow, that's amazing," I told Ross. "You're right: That's what that book is all about. What other books of the Bible have you read so far?"

"Well, Revelation—and Matthew, Mark, Luke, and John."

Ross then explained that he had realized eternity is the most important question we need to settle in this life, preferably while we're still young. "I was an atheist all the way through school," he confided. "After high school, though, I didn't want to go to college. Instead, I signed up to serve my country. My gig is guarding the Portland International Airport. See these fatigues? I'm wearing a big fat sign that says, 'Shoot me first,' if a terrorist ever attacks the airport."

Ross ranted a bit about America's past and current failures, then picked up on a couple of the themes in Ecclesiastes and wove in his interpretations of Revelation. "I don't understand it all," he said, "but I'm convinced all this bad stuff is going to happen—probably in my lifetime."

Ross glanced out the window for a moment. I still hadn't figured him out—his views were pretty eclectic.

"You know," Ross continued, "I went to church as a boy, but I don't have much use for it. My mom made me go. She's crazy." Ross explained how his churchgoing mother had abused him verbally and emotionally during her volatile bipolar episodes. Fellow church members only further hurt and alienated Ross.

"I never understood all this stuff back then. Besides, the church has too checkered of a past. They've forgotten what Jesus was all about. You know, he was the perfect Son of God. He never hurt anyone. He never hated anyone. Instead, he died on the cross for our sins. He's changed my life. Not that I'm perfect; no one is." He pondered that last point, gazing out the window again.

"You're right," I said, affirming several things he'd said—including the fact that no one's perfect and that the church has hurt people.

"I think it's important to accept everyone the way they are," Ross continued. "I keep trying to explain all this to my old girlfriend—we're still friends, even though she's into Wicca. She keeps reminding me of the bad things the church did to witches in the past. That wasn't right."

"No, that wasn't right," I agreed.

My train stop had come into view. I didn't want to end our conversation, but it was now 6:40 p.m. and I was late for dinner. I stood up.

"My name's Ross," he said with his right hand extending out toward mine.

We shook hands, then he asked, "And what's your name?"

"David. Say, thanks for the conversation. Much appreciated."

My conversation with Ross is a vivid reminder that many today know they need God—but often want to find him on their own, apart from the church. Yet when they find God, they're zealous to tell others about him.

RACHEL'S STORY

If anyone has ever been hurt while working on staff at a church, it's my dear friend Rachel. Several years ago, Rachel and her husband had just settled down in a relatively new, friendly, growing church with a good preacher. They were invited to join a small group of leaders, including the lead pastor and his wife. Later that same year, Rachel entered seminary. The pastor was quite encouraging, and three years later when Rachel needed an internship, he invited her to join the church staff.

Rachel was in for a big shock. At the second staff meeting she attended, the pastor harshly criticized a young youth worker, and she ran from the room crying. Rachel looked around the room in disbelief. But the other staff members stood up quietly and stared out the windows. No one confronted the pastor. When they reconvened, it was as if nothing had transpired.

Rachel was incensed. She had studied abuse within churches at seminary, and there was no doubt she had just witnessed it. She decided to approach the pastor and explain as kindly as she could what she saw in his actions. His face immediately contorted with anger. Later another staff member told her, "The pastor has the memory of an elephant. He will never forget that you confronted him."

The months went by, and the church grew to almost nine hundred people. Rachel and her team created an innovative program to welcome new people, and the youth programs were thriving. But still, Monday morning staff meetings were tense. Rachel could feel the lead pastor's disdain. There was no freedom around that staff table. People laughed carefully, spoke guardedly, and after the meetings retreated into their separate cubicles.

Each staff member reacted differently to the pastor's attitude. Some pretended nothing was wrong. Others talked about it constantly. Others were deeply depressed, wondering if they should continue serving God in a church capacity. Rachel watched as these staff people were doubted, despised, and demoted privately and then exalted from the platform as the pastor announced their moving on to bigger and better things.

The pastor had convinced the elders that he was right. Most of them, wooed by his good preaching and blinded by his persuasive manner, believed that he was. No one paid much attention to the fact that he would not allow anyone close enough to him to hold him accountable, let alone speak prophetically to him about his life.

One day Rachel and her husband walked into her office, cleaned it out, and left a succinct letter of resignation under the pastor's door. The pastor had talked to Rachel roughly for the last time. He had also, very unwisely, written her e-mails that helped her verify to others some of what had transpired. Rachel had seen and heard and experienced enough abuse. Within a few hours they had left the city for a friend's home.

Rachel knew she would be accused of gossip if she talked about the situation, so she did not answer her phone for weeks.

She did not respond to the many cards and letters, in which friends and church members asked questions and pleaded with her to come back.

Although she was greatly freed from the invisible chains of fear that had bound her for months, grief and worry became Rachel's companions. Where would she attend church now? Could she ever trust Christian leaders again? When would she stop grieving over the people she had shepherded?

Rachel recalls, "Jesus Christ and my dear husband kept reminding me that God's world is big. God had not abandoned me. The life experiences, the gifts, the training, and the education he had so evidently woven into my becoming *me* would not be in vain. I was to wait in his presence, allow his healing to come and continue to come, work on forgiving, accept forgiveness, knock on new doors . . . and begin again."

God has since moved Rachel into much broader fields. She found a grace-filled church where her gifts are fully accepted and staff members talk openly and honestly and laugh heartily, a place where leaders are accountable to one another and refuge is afforded for all. For Rachel, it has been a place of healing, refreshment, and renewed vision.

Awakening to our calling as God's new prophets to the church

FAITH BUILDER

GOD'S NEW CHRIST-INSPIRED PROPHETS

If anyone has ever known the pain of religious hypocrisy, abuse, and worse . . . ironically, it was Jesus Christ. That God's Son would endure such wickedness is almost beyond belief.

A few weeks ago I was hiking with my friend Jim through

the picturesque wilderness on the Washington State side of the Columbia River Gorge. As we were walking along the narrow trail through the woods, Jim asked what it meant that Jesus emptied himself.

Jim was referring to the apostle Paul's description of Jesus from Philippians 2:7, which says that Jesus "gave up his divine privileges," or (more literally) "emptied" himself.

Jim remarked that he had a professor who said that the original meaning behind the term translated "emptied" meant being poured into something. The term was used to describe pouring wine into a goblet or pouring milk into a jug.

"I had never heard it explained that way before," Jim said. "But I've thought about it quite a few times since then."

As we walked, I pondered what Jim had said.

I wonder if the container Jesus was poured into was labeled "Prophet." In ancient times, biblical prophets were often called into that role around the age of thirty. We see this in Joseph's life. He was about that age when he foretold the fate of two of Pharaoh's staff members and later interpreted two of Pharaoh's disturbing dreams. The same is true of Ezekiel, who first started seeing visions of God and the future in his thirtieth year.

Despite the popularity of fortune cookies and horoscopes, I find most people don't really want to know what the future holds. Mostly, we're afraid to face the truth.

The movie *Stranger than Fiction* describes the power of the words "Little did he know." It's a literary device that is used when you have an omniscient narrator. But as great writers like Madeleine L'Engle and others have said openly, they're not all-knowing when they write a novel. The characters take on a life of their own. Sometimes new characters show up that the authors weren't expecting.

Contrary to popular belief, great writers and prophets don't know everything. But writers know enough to keep writing. And prophets know enough to say exactly what God tells them, even though they don't always know what it means.

When Jesus poured himself out, into a bottle, as it were, he was still fully God. He knew what characters were going to show up next. He knew what everything meant. But he still relied on God the Father to tell him what to say. I understand that to mean Jesus had the self-control *not* to tell everything he knew. He deliberately withheld information at every turn in the Gospel narratives, even though we have a whole list of reasons to believe he knew what the real score was. This was true right up to his crucifixion.

What's the point of telling the truth if people aren't ready to hear, believe, and die for it?

I've often marveled at the divine prerogative to withhold the truth, the facts, and the information that would help people make sense of what's happening in the moment or what will happen next.

But Hebrews 11:1 says faith is "the confidence that what we hope for will actually happen."

If God put all the cards on the table ahead of time and dealt all the cards around the table for every hand, we'd know exactly what to bid every time. We'd bet all our chips at just the right times, knowing without a shadow of a doubt that in the end we'd win big.

Ultimately, however, such knowledge would be a fatal poison to our souls. First, life would be meaningless. Second, faith would be impossible. Third, we'd stagger at the sheer magnitude of what we knew.

Finally, we would go mad over being shut out of all possibility of joy, hope, and love. Only when we embrace the cardinal virtues can God truly actualize his calling in our lives.

You and I may not want to believe that God calls us to be his prophets to the church for the twenty-first century. Yet no matter how much the church has wounded us, its only hope is a new generation of prophets who re-embrace faith, joy, and love; experience God's healing power; and demonstrate the reality that Christlike actions speak loudest with true words.

Prophetic words. Passionate words. Powerful, grace-filled words.

Words that echo the one who is not afraid to pour out his Spirit into us, and through us, to others.

Have you started experiencing God's healing power in your life? Are you willing to entertain the possibility that God wants to speak in and through you? I deeply and sincerely hope so.

My prayer for you when, by God's power and for his glory, you begin to embark on this dangerous new journey is this:

May God fulfill every good purpose of yours and every act prompted by your faith (based on 2 Thessalonians 1:11).

EPILOGUE

I ALWAYS WONDERED how Jesus convinced Peter, Andrew, James, John, and others to drop everything, leave it all behind, and start following him—with no stated destination, spelled-out itinerary, or promise of safe passage or return.

Exactly how did Jesus pull that off? While reading Mark's Gospel recently, I discovered the answer. First, Jesus came to their town. Second, he hung around with them for a number of days. Third, without warning, he disappeared.

Peter and the others looked for Jesus everywhere. Finally, they found him away from town and in the wilderness, walking stick in hand, ready for a long day's journey.

"Don't you know everyone has been looking for you?" Peter asked.

Jesus' reply, in essence, was this: "Yes, but we need to be going. I have many other towns to visit." It was clear there was no point trying to convince Jesus to come back. He was already standing up and starting down the road.

In that instant, Peter and the others had a decision to make. Jesus wasn't laying out various options. By his very actions, he was issuing a command.

The fact that the command was preceded by his absence no longer strikes me as strange.

What if the Lord sometimes disappears on purpose? What if God, by his very actions, is commanding us to get more serious about following him in a whole new, radically different, risking-everything, not-sure-where-this-is-going sort of way?

What is your experience to this point?

Has God ever given you the slip?

What's your story?

CORRESPONDENCE

THANK YOU so much for reading *If God Disappears*.

You may have found that this wasn't an easy book to read, but through various stories you have had an opportunity to get to know me a bit. Now I'd love the privilege of meeting you via e-mail (and perhaps in person someday when I'm speaking at an event in your area).

I'm open to hearing your take on what I've said in this book, whether you strongly agree or strongly disagree with it. I welcome the opportunity to hear your story, listen to your comments, field your questions, and discuss your concerns.

You can join the discussion at www.IfGodDisappears.org (or .com) or at www.IfGodDisappears.blogspot.com, where you can post your comments about this book and more.

I hope you'll take a few minutes to write me at IfGodDisappears@gmail.com as soon as you close this book.

And, finally, please don't put this book on a shelf. Instead, loan or give it to a friend.

www.IfGodDisappears.org
www.IfGodDisappears.blogspot.com
IfGodDisappears@gmail.com

ACKNOWLEDGMENTS

MY DEEP THANKS to everyone who shared their stories with me and gave me permission to retell them in this book. Your stories have changed my life.

My thanks to Greg Johnson, who first believed in this book, and to Tim Beals, who shared my vision for this book with Tyndale House Publishers.

My thanks to John Van Diest, Janis Long Harris, Lisa Jackson, Bonne Steffen, and the rest of Doug Knox's team at Tyndale. I couldn't have asked for a better group of people!

My thanks to everyone on my *If God Disappears* editorial review committee, whose critiques of early drafts of each chapter proved invaluable.

My thanks to Elizabeth Jones and Elizabeth Honeycutt, my editorial director and managing editor at Sanford Communications, Inc. Without your hard work, this book would have been twice as long and six months late. My thanks to Rebekah Clark, Alyssa Hoekman, Robin Banks, Beyth Hogue, and Amanda Bird for all you contributed to help make this book a reality.

My thanks to the more than fifty men and women who made up my *If God Disappears* prayer team. Please continue praying that God will use this book to change lives for his glory, honor, and praise.

My sincere thanks to my wife, Renée, for journeying through life with me for more than twenty-five years. You've shown me what it means to ask the right questions, listen intently, offer unconditional love, and never lose hope that God can transform someone's story. Your example, encouragement, support, and prayers have meant the world to me.

My sincere thanks to my oldest daughter and son-in-law, Elizabeth and Bill; to my second-oldest daughter and new son-in-law, Shawna and Jordan; and to my older son, Jonathan. Since your early childhoods, it's been my prayer that you would love God with all your heart, soul, strength, and mind—and love others as yourself. God has answered that prayer in such remarkable ways in each of your lives. I thank God for you every day.

My sincere thanks to my younger son, Benjamin, and youngest daughter, Annalise, who did their best to entertain and humor me while I was writing this book. I can't stop thanking God for both of you.

My deepest thanks to God, who wasn't afraid to disappear from my life. I had no idea what you were doing, but you did. In the end, you revolutionized my life.

NOTES

CHAPTER 1: UNSOLVED MYSTERIES

1. See http://www.americanbuddhist.net/general/thought-0?page=6 (viewed October 25, 2007).
2. This statement originally appeared in French in *Nouvel Observateur*. It first appeared in English in *National Review*, June 11, 1982, 677.
3. Luis Palau and David Sanford, *God Is Relevant* (New York: Doubleday, 1997), xi-xiii, tells Jean-Paul Sartre's story in more detail.
4. If, like Lisa, you long for healing from the wounds of child sexual abuse, I highly recommend *In the Wildflowers* produced by Restoring the Heart Ministries, www.rthm.cc/Wildflowers.
5. See http://www.csec.org/csec/sermon/yancey_3302.htm (viewed June 1, 2008).

CHAPTER 2: BEFORE A FALL

1. Bill Thrall, Bruce McNicol, and Ken McElrath, *The Ascent of a Leader* (San Francisco: Jossey-Bass, 1999), 91-94, tells Vincent van Gogh's story in more detail.

CHAPTER 3: ANYTHING GOES

1. Harold Kushner, *Who Needs God* (New York: Simon & Schuster, 1989), 82–83.
2. Bertrand Russell, *The Collected Works of Bertrand Russell, Vol 10* (London: Routledge), 192.
3. Aldous Huxley, *Ends and Means* (New York: Harper, 1937), 267.
4. Mark Twain, *Follow the Equator* (1897; repr., Whitefish, Montana: Kessinger Publishing, 2004), 146.
5. Ravi Zacharias, *A Shattered Visage* (Grand Rapids, Mich.: Baker Book House, 1990), 136.
6. J. P. Moreland and Kai Nielsen, *Does God Exist?* (Nashville, Tenn.: Thomas Nelson Publishers, 1990), 36.
7. Kai Nielsen, *God and the Grounding of Morality* (Ottawa: University of Ottawa Press, 1997), 13.
8. Zacharias, *A Shattered Visage*, 32.
9. Kushner, *Who Needs God?*, 22.
10. Palau and Sanford, *God Is Relevant*, 179–186, explores this subject in much more depth.

CHAPTER 6: LOST IN THOUGHT

1. Paul C. Vitz, *Faith of the Fatherless* (Dallas: Spence Publishing Company, 2000).
2. Palau and Sanford, *God Is Relevant*, 187.
3. Ibid.
4. Scott Larsen, editor, *Indelible Ink* (Colorado Springs: WaterBrook Press, 2003), 185.
5. Ibid., 222.

6. Ian C. Bradley, *The Call to Seriousness: The Evangelical Impact on the Victorians* (New York: Macmillan Publishing Co., 1976), especially the last chapter.

7. *850 Words of Relevant* (an e-newsletter published by *Relevant* magazine), September 10, 2002, 1.

8. Spencer Burke, *Out of the Ooze* (Colorado Springs: NavPress, 2007), 148.

CHAPTER 7: WHY ME?

1. You can read more of Dr. Garry Friesen's story at http://blogs.multnomah.edu/FriesenFortnightly.

2. See Andrew Coffin's review, "Sophie's Choice," *World*, March 25, 2006, 12.

SCRIPTURE INDEX

Matthew 2:1-12
Luke 22:66–23:25
Romans 9:8
Galatians 4:28
Joshua 21:45
Joshua 23:14
1 Kings 8:56
1 Kings 11:1-13
2 Peter 1:4
Joshua 1:5
Hebrews 13:5
2 Peter 3:9
Titus 1:2
Matthew 7:7
Genesis 1–3
Isaiah 53:5
Zephaniah 1:12
John 1:11-12
Luke 2:1-20
Luke 2:21-35
Acts 1:4-5
Ephesians 1:13-14
Psalm 23

CHAPTER 6

John 8:32
Philippians 4:7
Mark 12:30
Luke 10:27
Ephesians 6:4
Psalm 42:5

CHAPTER 7

Job
Isaiah 40:12
Exodus 7–12
Romans 8:31
John 3:16
1 John 3:1
Genesis 37
Romans 15:4

Romans 5
James 1
1 Peter 3:13-22
Genesis 1–36
Genesis 44–45
Romans 12:18
Isaiah 61:1-3

CHAPTER 8

Judges
Judges 13:1
Judges 13
2 Chronicles 7:14
2 Chronicles 7:19-20
John 3:16
Galatians 4:4
Psalm 103:13-14
Luke 15:11-32
Luke 15:20
Luke 15:21
1 Peter 3:15
1 Peter 3:1, 9-10
Exodus 20:1-17
Psalm 118
Matthew 6:33
Luke 12:31

CHAPTER 9

Luke 23:32-43
2 Chronicles 6–7
Philippians 2:7
Genesis 40–41
Ezekiel 1:1
Hebrews 11:1
2 Thessalonians 1:11

EPILOGUE

Mark 1:14-39